ARE YOU POSITIVE?

A Daily Guide to Breaking the Chains of Negativity & Achieving Success

John H. Perry

Copyright © 2022 John H. Perry

All rights reserved. No part of this book may be reproduced, stored in a retrieval system, or transmitted, in any form or by any means (electronic, mechanical, photocopying, recording, or otherwise), without prior written permission from the publisher, except in the case of brief quotations in articles or reviews.

Cover design by Vila Design

Published by Van Rye Publishing, LLC
Ann Arbor, MI
www.vanryepublishing.com

ISBN: 979-8-9851099-8-6 (paperback)
ISBN: 979-8-9851099-9-3 (ebook)
Library of Congress Control Number: 2022933305

Dedication

To the little children of the world who still believe they can do anything. You can!

Contents

Preface   vii

Introduction   ix

PART I: DAYS 1–100
- Days 1–25   1
- Days 26–50   26
- Days 51–75   51
- Days 76–100   76

PART II: DAYS 101–200
- Days 101–125   103
- Days 126–150   128
- Days 151–175   153
- Days 176–200   178

PART III: DAYS 201–300
- Days 201–225   205
- Days 226–250   230
- Days 251–275   255
- Days 276–300   281

PART IV: DAYS 301–366
- Days 301–325   309
- Days 326–350   334
- Days 351–366   359

Conclusion   375

About the Author   379

Preface

OUR SOCIETY IS INUNDATED with negativity—so much so that we have become accustomed to it. We now accept some negative as positive, if it conforms to our preconceived opinions.

For example: you are watching a network news show, and it is critical of the political party or candidate you like. As a result, you perceive the network as negative. You change channels to a different network's show that is covering the party or candidate of the opposition, and the show is being critical of them. As a result, you consider the network as being positive. Why? Because the second network is in agreement with your views. However, *both* network shows are being negative!

Just because a negative agrees with your views does not necessarily mean it is a positive. And if we consistently accept negative input—regardless of whether it agrees or disagrees with our views—then we begin to think in a negative light! That is why I wrote this book, as a daily study in positive thinking. I wrote it mostly for myself, but hopefully, it will help you too.

Please accept the contents of this book as a way to change your attitudes and see the world in a more positive light.

—John H. Perry

Introduction

IN A REAL SENSE, our world is not the physical reality around us but rather how we perceive the world and how we perceive what goes on around us. I am not being an eastern mystic; I am being realistic about how each of us mentally processes what we see and hear and relates that to our reality. When we misinterpret our observations because we have a negative attitude, this is what Zig Ziglar called "stinking thinking." How you think will affect how you perceive the world around you, and soon, you will be deceiving yourself about what is actually going on in your life.

I am sure any police officer could support me—in a sense—in seeing how witnesses to a common accident or event can give widely different accounts of what happened. For example, witnesses might describe a vehicle as being different colors or going in different directions, or one person identifies the driver as a man while another says it was a woman, and on and on. In many cases, the witness statements leave the investigators with such discrepancies that the investigators are unsure who or what they are actually looking for.

The reason for the witness discrepancies is how the witnesses processed what they saw and related it to their concept of reality. The same applies in all aspects of daily life, including our very personal relationships. Many marital arguments and issues are based on misunderstandings caused by differences in perception.

The much-used term "brainwashing" is simply manipulating someone to see things the way you want them to—in other words, to perceive the world in the reality you want them to—so that you can control their actions and reactions in any given situation. Brainwashing is not always the movie characterization of torture and threats; it can be as simple as repeated misinformation or emotional stress in a

Introduction

situation. Fear is a great way to implement brainwashing and condition people to react the way someone wants them to.

Usually, our negative thoughts lead us to have negative reactions and perceptions and allow other people to manipulate our actions. In contrast, positive thoughts and positive outlooks help us see things more realistically and clearly, and they make us less likely to be manipulated. Positive thoughts also make us happier, which makes us even *more* positive and breeds even *more* clear, realistic, and positive thinking. Soon, we are seeing life in a brighter and happier way—bad things are no longer so bad, and previously unseen opportunities begin to appear in life. We suddenly feel capable of taking on more challenges, success becomes the norm rather than failure, and failures are not a disaster but rather lessons learned and steps to success.

I know thinking positive seems like a Pollyanna outlook, but it is what the *real* norm is! All our lives, we have been fed so much negative through bad music, television, movies, news, etc. that we no longer think positive and seeing the world in a negative context seems normal. What I want to do in this book is help you reprogram your brain to think in positive mode and start perceiving your world in a positive way. I want to help you eliminate the toxic emotions, bad words, and negative reactive feelings that come to your mind automatically and instead start experiencing the positive.

There are a few words that we almost automatically think of in any new situation: can't, won't, hate, dislike, etc. These words cause us to avoid new people, new things, and new opportunities without ever giving them a chance. In this book, I hope to enlighten you to more positive approaches so that you will begin automatically thinking in terms of: can, will, like, okay, etc. Once you start doing so, a whole new world will open up for you.

As you read through the quotes that appear throughout this book, there might be a quote from someone you don't like or from a source you don't agree with. But I admonish you *not* to judge the wisdom

Introduction

or input of the quote based on the speaker. You can get motivation, wisdom, or knowledge from the most unlikely sources. I have often been chastised for speaking positively about successful people who have sordid personal lives, but their personal lives are not what I admire; it's their accomplishments and how they achieved them that are what I look at. You learn from their success what to do, and you learn from their personal failures what *not* to be! So, keep an open mind.

One request: please take this book one day at a time and let it sink in gradually, meditating on what it means to you, but don't forget the previous day as you move forward. Let the positivity build up by reading new ideas each day but repeating the ideas of the previous day so that you repeat and accumulate each positive idea presented in this book. It's like going to the gym: repetition pays BIG dividends! At times, you might feel that I am repeating some of the same points. And I am, in a way, but I am doing so based on different scenarios. You don't go to the gym and do one sit up and stop, thinking your abs are taken care of. Instead, repetitions and different ab workouts are necessary for development, and attitude change takes the same approach. Hang in there as you read this book at a pace of one page a day, and let time and consistency do their work.

PART I

~DAYS 1–100~

Day 1

"All things are possible if you only just believe!"

—Jesus

I once heard someone say, "If you believe you can, or if you believe you can't, you are right." Think about that. It is not "can" or "can't," it is what *you* believe about yourself!

I don't know where it came from in my life, but even as a teenager, it was almost like a dare that if someone said, "You can't do that"—meaning I was not capable of doing it—then I knew I was going to try. And people always told me that when you reached a certain age, things in life were over: "Boy, when you turn forty, things sure change for the worse." But I have instead approached each key age with a relish rather than a regret, and even though aging does have a physical effect, I don't let it have a mental effect.

Don't let other people dictate how you see opportunities or life. Think for yourself and be positive!

Day 2

"If you change your mindset, you have the ability to change your whole world."

—Damien Thomas

Yesterday, we said "believing" is important to positivity and success, and I am now telling you that it is the *essential* element. Regardless of how many positive thoughts you put in your mind, how many positive actions you take, or how many positive results you get, if you fail to believe in yourself and the results of a positive lifestyle, you will not succeed. So, always remember to believe!

Part I: Days 1–100

Day 3

> "Take a deep breath. It's just a bad day, not a bad life!"
>
> —Unknown

Have you ever noticed how your physical condition affects your perception of life? If you wake up feeling rested and well, then even a bad day is tolerable. But if you wake up sick and especially nauseous, then the best of days is miserable. It's not the day; it's how you feel!

I know it is hard to overcome illness and its effect on your feelings and attitude, but the way to begin is to start taking mindful control of the effect of your feelings on your day. Get up and make a conscious decision to have a positive outlook. Tell yourself that you will see the good in people and the bright side of every situation. You never know what the outcome is really going to be anyway, so why not try to assume that a bad break will lead to a good outcome?

Many times, in golf, I have hit a bad tee shot but ended up making par on the hole anyway. For you non-golfers, that's a good thing. So, a good result came from a bad start. Don't judge the end from the start!

Day 4

"Life goes on whether you choose to take a chance on the unknown or stay behind, locked in the past, thinking about what could have been."

—Anonymous

I read a story about Steve Jobs, who was a founder of Apple and creator of much of our most-used modern technology. It seems that after he built Apple to its greatness and developed the iPod, Apple's board of directors fired him. While "unemployed," Jobs developed some ideas on his own and came up with a new idea that caused Apple to rehire him as the CEO. That new idea—one which might not have come along if he had not been fired—was the iPhone!

You never know where adversity will lead. Don't quit just because you hit a bump in the road. If Jobs had given up and gone home to pout, we might not have smartphones today!

Part I: Days 1–100

Day 5

"Abraham was seventy-five years old and married to a barren woman. He believed God for twenty-five years before he saw the answer to God's promise in Isaac. The rest is history. Just believe!"

—John H. Perry

We are a fast-food society, expecting instant results. But often, the best things in life take time. Actually, most things that last take time to create. Too many people start out believing but quit after a brief time because they don't see the results they think they should see. But in many cases, they simply quit too soon to see those results!

My favorite story is about the giant bamboo tree. You plant the tree, and for five years you fertilize and water it and wait, and you see . . . nothing. Then, in the fifth year, it suddenly grows ninety feet high in about six weeks. For the first five years, the tree has been putting down a root system to support itself, and when everything is ready, boom, it grows.

In life, many things we want are like that. We have to fertilize, water, and wait until there is a solid base, and then things will develop. Be patient and keep believing. Your harvest is on the way!

Day 6

"Start your day with good intentions and a list, and finish with a completed list."

—John H. Perry

One of my biggest problems in life used to be not being organized and running randomly through the day. I had good intentions, but distractions kept me from accomplishing what I wanted to get done. Finally, I got some good advice: start the day with a positive attitude and a prioritized list of what you want to accomplish!

I found that having a list with my priorities kept me focused, and even when I had to deviate, I had a guide to get back on course and complete my goals. The greatest satisfaction was to finish the day with a positive attitude and a completed list. After a while, I found that most days, I finished my list early and was able to handle other tasks as well. Having the list, I could map my time and routes in an orderly manner and seldom had to backtrack.

Try making a prioritized list for a few days. You will see that you get things done and get them done better!

Day 7

"Forget the mistake but remember the lesson."

—Unknown

By now, you should be getting some idea of how positive thoughts and positive actions can change your world and your outlook. If you aren't getting a new view on life and getting more accomplished, maybe you are taking the wrong approach. Many positive lifestyle gurus promote "positive thinking." That's all well and good, but positive *thinking* alone is a passive approach. Positive thinking will get you nowhere if there is no positive *action*!

You have to "do" to accomplish. I know you are only six days into this book, but you should have been acting from day one. Do you start going to the gym to get in shape and for the first few weeks just sit on the bench staring at the equipment visualizing your new body and improved health? No! You start exercising from day one! The same applies here, and I hope you have been taking some positive *action*.

If you haven't been taking actual steps yet, start! If you have been taking actual steps, have you succeeded? If you haven't, I am happy for you because, as you will learn later on in this book, failure is a lesson that moves you closer to success.

Day 8

"Your mistakes don't define you!"

—Amy Wolff

If you haven't already made mistakes, you will—maybe a lot of them. But as yesterday's quote said, forget the mistake but remember the lesson. Remembering the lesson is a positive side of a mistake. Another positive side is that the mistake doesn't define you but "promotes" you.

The greatest geniuses in history made numerous mistakes before they achieved success. Stories go that Thomas Edison tried hundreds of ways to perfect the filament in the light bulb before he found one that worked reliably. Alexander Graham Bell tried many times before the phone worked. Every great invention has a history of failures leading to its success. However, no one remembers the failures; they just celebrate the end product.

You are the same. People will celebrate your end game and not remember your mistakes. Anyone who has risen in life without making a mistake is either a liar or hasn't been caught lying yet.

Day 9

> "It's not how many times you fall down. It's how many times you get back up!"
>
> —Unknown

The race of life isn't measured in terms of who comes in first. Instead, it's measured by who finishes the race. By that, I mean people who strive to reach the end, stay positive, contribute, and are a part of the whole. Too many people stop along the way and just quit living.

Negativity, fear, and letting others dictate their life takes many people out of the race of life long before it is over. They live in the same house on the same street in the same town for decades. The furniture is the same as forty years ago and is even in the same place in the house. Their environment is like a time machine, and their conversations are like one too.

Somewhere along the path, those people fell down, and they stayed there for the rest of life. Get back up and get back in the race!

Day 10

"Nothing is really hard if you break it down into smaller tasks."

—Mark Twain

Often, we face a challenge that overwhelms us because it seems too big for us to handle. We stare at the sheer size of the project and realize we can't do it. Instead of thinking of the components of the problem and how they are related and how to approach them one at a time, we instead become paralyzed by the overall monster.

The old joke question is, "How do you eat an elephant?" Answer: "One bite at a time!" Never let a huge problem overwhelm you. Instead, stop and look at it in its component parts and decide where you can start. Then, progress one step at a time to resolve the problem.

Part I: Days 1–100

Day 11

"All things are difficult before they become easy."
—Thomas Fuller

The human mind is a complex system of cells interlocked with synapses that send signals that are analyzed and stored. Tasks we practice are learned in many ways but most commonly through rote memory—or repetition learning. After you do something repeatedly over a certain period, you begin to almost do it automatically.

Years ago, I was a trainer for the US Postal Service, and I trained new employees who were going to carry mail, sort mail, and do other tasks. Every new person fretted over their ability to do the job because it seemed very complicated. I told them all to do two things. First, listen to their job trainer. Second, give themselves six weeks. I told them that if they would just hang in there for six weeks, they would be doing the job like they had been there for years.

With almost no exception, I was right about the six weeks. Many of my trainees would stop me on the work floor and tell me that they had almost quit but instead did what I said and stayed for six weeks. And by the time they had been there six weeks, it was almost like magic that they could do the job like the old hands could.

Six weeks is the time it takes to break or make a habit. Our brains are awesome things, and we just need to learn to get out of their way and let them do their job!

Day 12

"The things I want to know are in books. My best friend is the man who'll get me a book I ain't read."

—Abraham Lincoln

One of the best books I have ever read on being positive and taking positive action was written in the 1930s. It is called *Think and Grow Rich* by Napoleon Hill. I put off reading it for years because I assumed it was one of those gimmick books that promoted some woo-woo way to get rich quick. But when I finally read it, I was amazed at how realistic the ideas in it are.

The writer, Napoleon Hill, knew some of the great men of the early twentieth century, like Andrew Carnegie, and he wrote based on the business ideas that made them successful. I strongly recommend the book. And don't be initially put off by how he expresses himself and his ideas. He will pull it all together. One of the concepts that is really critical is the concept of teamwork. Today's lesson is simply that I recommend this book: *Think and Grow Rich* by Napoleon Hill.

Part I: Days 1–100

Day 13

"Shallow men believe in luck or in circumstance. Strong men believe in cause and effect."

—Ralph Waldo Emerson

Many people are superstitious and are nervous about the number thirteen and especially about Fridays that fall on the thirteenth of a month. Personally, I think superstition is silly, and Friday the 13th for me is a uniquely special day. Superstition attributes things to uncontrollable forces of mysticism, and for the positive and confident person, there is no room for superstitious beliefs!

In my life, Friday the 13th has played several positive roles. For example, my mother was born on a Friday the 13th, my brother was born on a Friday the 13th, and I joined the Army (a positive event in my life) on a Friday 13th! When I was on jump status at Fort Bragg, I scheduled a jump on a Friday the 13th and placed myself on the thirteenth aircraft as the thirteenth man, and we jumped at 1,300 feet. It was the best jump I ever had!

Don't let mysticism or superstition invade your thinking. It will cripple your success.

Day 14

"Be stronger than your best excuse."
—Unknown

It's so easy to come up with excuses why you can't do something or why there is not enough time to do it. Somehow, we always have time to watch three or four hours of mindless television, or we can do something that we enjoy, like a five-hour round of golf. And yet, we convince ourselves that there is no time to do what's important for our future!

I think I have heard almost every excuse possible in some variation or another, and I am about fed up with the words "I can't." Usually, the words "I can't" really mean "I don't want to take the time to" or "I don't want to take the time to figure out how." Most of the time, it is simply that you have not done it before, and so you do not want to try it now.

As a manager and leader in the Army, I would get angry when I heard the response, "I can't." I took it as a personal challenge to show the person they were wrong! The funny part was that, after I showed them they could, most of them became dynamos and enthusiastic to take on more because it stimulated their sense of accomplishment and self-worth to realize what they could really do. It paid dividends for me because I had units that increased efficiency, and the "I *can*" attitude bred new enthusiasm in others in the unit. Success breeds success!

Day 15

"Sometimes later becomes never. Do it now!"

—Napoleon Hill

Just like making excuses, procrastination can destroy success. I used to be a pro at procrastination. My wife's favorite word was "procrastinator," and it was always directed at me! I know, here I am writing this positive book, and I am admitting to this key fault. Well, we all have a sordid past.

The problem with putting things off is that you can take it to extremes, and things have a way of adding up. Soon, you have a mountain of things to do, and you are overwhelmed. Then, you start focusing on eliminating what you canNOT do so that you can get the pile to a manageable size, and that is not a good thing.

Take my learned advice: do not put off what you can do now! Just as I advised earlier, keep a list and work it down every day. If possible, start each day with a blank slate.

Day 16

"If you can Imagine it, you can achieve it. If you can dream it, you can become it."

—William Arthur Ward

Most of my life, I have had a dream of being a published author. I have written hundreds of stories and started dozens of books. I have wanted to impact other people's lives in some manner through my writing and be a "writer." For one reason or another, I never reached that dream. But . . .

You are holding the completion of that dream in your hands! I have become the dream. I imagined what I wanted to write and what it would do. I set my mind to accomplishing it and took the advice I read from someone else and made writing a job. I spent time every day working at it to accomplish it. I dreamed about it and kept it fresh in my mind. And now . . . I am it!

Positive thoughts, positive actions, and positive outcomes. If you read *Think and Grow Rich*—as I suggested on Day 12—you will see what Napoleon Hill talked about as something being created from nothing by your thoughts. That is exactly how the book in your hand came about. One day the book was only a thought in my mind, and now, it is a tangible, material item in your hands.

Day 17

"The dumbest question is the one you don't ask."

—Anonymous drill sergeant

Have you ever been in a classroom or at a lecture or forum, and the speaker asks if there are any questions, and you have one, but you are reluctant to raise your hand because you think it is a dumb question? So, you wait, hoping someone else will ask it. But no one does, and you leave wondering what the answer is.

Somewhere else in that room, there were others with that same question, and they didn't ask it either for the same reason you didn't. And they wonder what the answer is, too. And maybe, just maybe, you and one or more of them have failed to achieve success or been delayed because you didn't get that answer. Maybe it wasn't a dumb question after all!

If you have a question, ask it. It doesn't matter what anyone else thinks because the answer might be the breakthrough you need. Even if the question seems dumb, down the road, it might be the key to unlocking some other question that you cannot imagine now.

Take the advice I received from a drill sergeant one dark morning on a rifle range: "The only dumb question is the one you don't ask!"

Day 18

"If you don't ask, the answer is always no."

—Unknown

While we are on the subject of questions, there is something else you need to know. People cannot read your mind, and they are not all grinches just waiting to make your life miserable.

All too often, we have a question—sometimes about a need—and we get it in our mind that if we ask the person that can answer that question or meet that need, they will refuse us or think we are imposing or that we are incompetent for not handling it ourselves. I have been there myself. You start imagining the reactions, and before long, you talk yourself out of asking. That is one reason I never authored a book before. It's because I wouldn't submit a manuscript, figuring I would be rejected. I was rejected three times on my first novel, and I never tried again.

Zig Ziglar said every no is one step closer to a yes. That isn't just in sales; that's in life. Never not ask!

Day 19

"Set your mind on a definite goal and observe how quickly the world stands aside to let you pass."

—Napoleon Hill

People who are focused and concentrated on a project are usually left alone by most other people. It quickly becomes obvious to others that the person has a goal in life and that other activities are of little or no interest to them. The athlete who wants to make the Olympics or get a scholarship or go to the pros will practice beyond what others do. They will skip the extracurricular activities like partying and will get their rest, be up early training, and train when others have finished. Many have limited or no social life due to their focused goals.

When the focused person succeeds in life, many people say things like: "They were blessed with natural talent" or "they got all the breaks." But the fact is that they *made* the breaks happen, and they developed the talent through long hours of hard work and dedicated practice!

Whatever your goal—athletic, business, or whatever—you will have to make short-term sacrifices to achieve long-term gains. Are you willing to do so? If you are, the world will step aside and let you move to the head of the class in whatever field you endeavor!

Day 20

"The way of success is the way of continuous pursuit of knowledge."

—Napoleon Hill

When I quit high school to join the Army, my school counselor surprised me. He said I was making a good decision because I was bored in school. But he made me promise one thing: that I would not stop learning and pursuing my education. He told me about the GED tests and said that I should also take night classes and work toward a college degree. I promised him I would.

After I reached my first Army assignment location, one of the first things I did was locate the education office and inquire about opportunities. As a result, I had my high school equivalency before my friends graduated high school, and I was taking college classes before they graduated as well. I stuck with it, and I graduated college *magna cum laude* while on active duty and attended numerous military schools as well. The Army was my chosen profession, and I studied it and became very good at it during my career, and I was on several occasions assigned to teach at its schools.

Never stop learning and never pass up a chance to learn something new!

Part I: Days 1–100

Day 21

"We refuse to believe that which we don't understand."

—Napoleon Hill

All through the ages, this has been one of humankind's biggest problems! People refuse to believe what they don't understand. If it weren't for a few open-minded adventurers, willing to go beyond the limits, we'd probably still be in caves in northern Europe looking at the Atlantic Ocean and wondering what was on the other side or if there was another side at all.

Every great advancement—from fire to the internet—has been resisted by the establishment out of fear and ignorance. So, don't look at life as a great mystery that can't be solved. Instead, look at it as a mystery that you want to solve. Sometime in the nineteenth century, the head of the US Patent Office declared that they should close shop because anything that could be invented had already been invented. Boy, was he wrong! There is always something new or some new way to do something waiting to be discovered.

Let your mind loose in the cosmos and see what you can discover that no one else can see!

Day 22

"Give me six hours to chop down a tree, and I will spend the first four sharpening the ax."

—Abraham Lincoln

Old Abe knew that the real secret to a successful venture is proper preparation! Probably from experience, he knew that a dull ax would lead to a long and tiring day cutting trees and most likely a not-so-productive day. In addition to sharpening the ax before starting, he would also stop occasionally and re-sharpen the edge to keep it at its best after starting.

Too often, we get all excited about an idea or project and leap into it without proper preparation, and soon, we grow frustrated, disillusioned, and lose interest. If we had taken time to evaluate what was needed and do our prep work, we could have been successful and accomplished our goal. Many goals will require us to take courses or spend time on research or even put together a team of knowledgeable assistants to accomplish the goal. We have to develop patience about starting and about the preparation.

Always take time to sharpen your ax!

Part I: Days 1–100

Day 23

"Those who are crazy enough to think they can change the world usually do."

—Steve Jobs

Jobs should know; he was one of the modern wizards who changed society through technology. Hardly anyone in the world doesn't use something he inspired or created. Smartphones, regardless of brand, can be traced back to him. He created the first one, and all others are spin-offs.

Likewise, Apple Computers started the revolution for personal home computers. Without Jobs's hardware to stimulate the growth, there wouldn't have been much of a market for Bill Gates's software to build on. And people like Columbus, Galileo, and Newton were considered crazy in their time and were ridiculed for their ideas. But their ideas changed society and the world as they knew it.

There is so much more left that you can do! Just get outside the box and look around.

Day 24

"Ambition is not what a man would do but what a man does, for ambition without action is fantasy."

—Bryant McGill

Ambition without action is daydreaming. As McGill said, it is fantasy! There is no telling how many great ideas, great inventions, or great philosophies have been imagined but, because the person who imagined them just laid on the couch, never came to pass.

I am guilty of that myself. I invented several things in my youth, but they never got past a drawing I placed in my drawer. Years later, I saw them advertised in a magazine. Someone else had the same (almost identical) ideas and took action and made money from them!

You might have the greatest idea there has ever been in history, but if that is all it ever is, it is nothing. The process is to have a vision or idea, put it in writing or drawing, then take action and create it. Otherwise, it is just a fantasy!

Early on in this book, I suggested you read *Think and Grow Rich*. In that book, the author talks about the process of how the great tycoons of their day created empires from their dreams. It's not magic; it takes work. The book you hold in your hand is such a thing. It started as a vision in my mind, and then I did the research, the preparation, and the writing work, and then got it published. And now you hold the manifested vision. It works!

Day 25

"Our ambitions can only be limited by our doubts."

—Rajesh

The only person—I say again the *only* person—who can stop your dreams is *you*! And that will come from your doubts.

There is a verse in the Bible where Jesus is talking to a father who wants his son healed but is suffering from doubt. The words Jesus speaks are the key to all of life's success: "All things are possible if you only just believe."

Just believe! So simple but so deep. Doubt is the destroyer of dreams and ambition. Doubt crushes faith. The sad part is that it can happen to any one of us if we aren't careful.

Don't doubt your dreams. Believe in yourself! You will encounter problems, but they aren't final; they are just bumps in the road. Just *believe*!

Day 26

"Intelligence without ambition is a bird without wings."

—Walter H. Cottingham

Years ago, I worked in the circulation department at a newspaper, which is the department where carriers work. We had to deliver papers in the morning, and we picked them up at the dock at 2 a.m. The rural delivery people would gather there waiting for the papers so they could get an early start, and it was a fascinating collection of people from all walks of life.

There was one man who I remember would sit on the sidewalk reading and seldom talked. Another carrier told me the man was a genius with a very high IQ but that he had never done anything but deliver papers. He had dropped out of college and started a route, and for more than twenty years, that was all he'd done. All that potential intelligence wasted—a bird without wings!

It is better to have an average or below-average intelligence but be willing to work at something and study and put forth effort than a genius who sits on the couch watching TV and dreaming. Most successful businessmen are not overly intelligent, but they are willing to work, and they have ambition.

Be ambitious regardless of how intelligent you are!

Day 27

"Teamwork is the ability to work together toward a common vision. It is the fuel that allows common people to attain uncommon results."

—Andrew Carnegie

In *Think and Grow Rich*, the idea of teamwork to achieve a goal is one of the main concepts that Napoleon Hill presents. It was the keystone to the success of great tycoons like Carnegie, Rockefeller, and others of their era. They knew that they didn't know it all and couldn't do it all, so they surrounded themselves with others who could round them out. If I recall, Hill referred to it as the "mastermind" concept.

You might start out alone, but you will soon find that you need other people to round you out. You will need others' expertise. You will need managers, advisers, financial managers, personnel directors, etc. You can't and shouldn't try to do it all yourself.

At the same time, you should share your success with the others and make them a part of the dream as it motivates them to *become* a part of it. When you grow tired, they will encourage you. Create the team that compliments you, but make sure there is diversity so that there is freshness of outlook. If everyone always agrees, you will be stale!

Day 28

"The key is to keep company only with people who uplift you, whose presence calls forth your best."

—Epictetus

At all costs, avoid the naysayers. You need someone who will bring up alternatives and point out when you or the project may be deviating, but you don't need a negative nanny! If anyone is always telling you that it can't be done, you need to gently get rid of them. You will have enough struggle in the natural course of events that you don't need a negative voice always in your ear.

When I was the commander of a Special Forces A-Team, I had one sergeant I encouraged to feel free to approach me if he thought I was off track because I respected his opinion and military record. But I told him to do it discreetly and know that I might take his comment and ignore it anyway. Even if I did, I wanted his input because I did not think I knew all the answers. On quite a few occasions, he made a difference, and he once kept me from going way off course on a patrol. He was not a negative person; he was a positive input who helped me—there's a difference.

The naysayer will always find something wrong and will always predict doom and gloom. He or she will ruin the team's morale and discourage your efforts. Stay around positive people—the kind who, in the midst of a total failure, look for a positive solution!

Day 29

"Small-minded people blame others. Average people blame themselves. The wise see all blame as foolishness."

—Epictetus

This is important! The blame game can destroy a team, create bad morale, and shatter a dream. So, don't blame. Instead, take responsibility if you are at fault but also move on. Once something is done, it is done.

If someone maliciously created a problem, handle it in private and, if necessary, terminate them. But don't run around blaming. Analyze what happened, discuss it with your team, figure out how to correct it, and . . . *move on*! Emphasize the learning points and make it as positive a situation as you can.

If someone on your team is blaming themself, take them aside and comfort them, talk about it, and let them know you forgive any carelessness—or whatever the issue was—and that you want to move on in good faith. Usually, this will build a stronger team.

Day 30

"Do your duty and a little more and the future will take care of itself."

—Andrew Carnegie

So many people show up and do the minimum at work and complain about not getting a raise or promotion. I hear people say, "If they pay me more, I will do more!" Sorry guys, but that's not how it works. They are already paying you for an eight-hour day, and you probably aren't even giving them that. So, why would they pay you more to get less?

Bosses look at what you do, and they promote and give pay raises based on your value. I once had a co-worker say, "They have to pay me what I am worth." I responded, "I agree, but they do have to pay you something." He didn't like my answer!

When you go to work, put in what you are paid to do and then a little more. In time, your superiors will see your effort and promote you or give you a raise or both. If they don't in a reasonable time, then go ask for it. If they still don't, then go find a better employer! Most of the time, they won't let you go.

When you are pursuing your dream, pay yourself the same way. Put in your best and then some!

Day 31

> "All human beings can alter their lives by altering their attitudes."
>
> —Andrew Carnegie

You are going to hear that a lot in this book in one form or the other! Your attitude or outlook is how your world will be. Two people walk into a room at the same time and see and hear the same people. Depending on their attitude, they react to the environment in different ways.

One of the people who walked in has a negative outlook, so they are expecting things to be bad. To them, the room is too crowded, they don't like the people, the people are too noisy, and the room is too hot or too cold. They don't want to be there, and they don't want to socialize.

The other person who walked in is in a positive mood, so they are expecting good things. For them, there is a good mixture of people they like, and the music is great. The room is comfortable, and they are looking forward to socializing with the people in the room. This is going to be a great night!

What's the difference? Attitude! If either person changes their attitude, their environment changes. *You* are in control of your environment. You don't like the way things are? Then simply change your attitude about the environment and the things in it!

Day 32

"It is the mind that makes the body rich."

—Andrew Carnegie

Wow! This can go in so many directions! Just like yesterday's discussion about attitude, your mind can affect you and your body in so many ways. Your health and how you feel can be affected by your mind so easily.

If you dwell on feeling bad and imagine you have aches and pains or are feeling symptoms of an illness, you can literally begin to feel sick. Hypochondriacs are people who can actually make themselves sick by believing they are sick. Or people can drive themselves insane by thinking insane things and by thinking that they *are* insane.

The good news is that, on another angle, your mind can motivate you to be creative and literally obtain wealth by starting businesses or coming up with new ideas or inventions, etc. The mind controls everything for you!

The big thing to me is that the mind lets me explore the world through reading, watching, and imagination. I am rich in knowledge and creativity!

Part I: Days 1–100

Day 33

"People rarely succeed unless they have fun in what they are doing."

—Andrew Carnegie

So many people fail to consider this when they are deciding on a career! They look at what is lucrative financially or popular in society, but they do not consider how they will *feel* doing a job or profession. They go to college for four, six, eight, or more years, get out, and finally go to work, and in a few months, they realize, *I hate this job!*

I knew a guy who was a successful computer guy with IBM and making great money. But he hated his job! He started taking classes to be an auto mechanic, quit IBM, and went to work in a little auto shop in an out-of-the-way place. Suddenly, he *loved* what he did! He never regretted taking a step down in pay or what others considered a step down in prestige. He was . . . *happy!*

If you don't enjoy what you are doing, you won't give it your best. Your dream is what you love. Follow your dream; you'll never regret it!

Day 34

"When your ambition is greater than your fear, your life will get bigger than your dream."

—Farshad Asl

All too often, we are afraid to try! That's the only problem—fear stops us from trying. The funny thing is, there are two sides to the fear. Fear of failure is the obvious side. But the surprising one is fear of success.

Failure scares us because we think it is a sign we can't do it, and so we give up. Fear of success is the odd one because with success comes responsibility—the responsibility to keep on and to manage the success. What are we going to do with what we accomplished, and will it dominate our lives, and will we have to change to control it, or will it control us?

Too often, we haven't taken the time to think about the future results of our ambition and what we want if we achieve it. When we do start to think about that, and we decide that it is what we really want, then the fear can be controlled—even vanquished. And then, our ambition will take us to heights we never imagined!

Day 35

"There is hope in dreams, in imagination, and in the courage of those who wish to make those dreams a reality."

—Jonas Salk

In all of history, only a small handful of people have really moved mankind forward in civilization. The vast majority of people have been followers, content to sit back and observe or settle where they are and live out their lives. Others resisted change outright.

I once read that, at one point in time, only 13–15 percent of colonists supported the revolutionists in the fight for freedom from England. A very small minority led to the US being the US. The people who have explored, invented, and created are a tiny minority of civilization, but they have made a massive impact on the majority!

Salk is the man who created the Polio vaccine that stopped the disease from crippling and killing people worldwide. One man's efforts reached the world. You might be the next one to touch the world, so have the courage to pursue your dreams!

Day 36

"Everybody likes a compliment."

—Abraham Lincoln

At one time in my life, I worked for the US Postal Service, and one of my duties was checking in mail carriers as they returned for the day. I knew many of them and knew their efforts to do a good job, so on occasion, I liked to compliment them.

One day, a particular carrier who was known to be a grumpy old man but a good carrier came in, and I complimented him. As he turned to walk away, he stopped and looked back at me with a funny look on his face and said, seriously and almost sadly, "I've been here over twenty-five years, and that's the first time anyone thanked me for doing my job." I almost cried.

People like being complimented, and they deserve to be complimented when they do a good job. Studies have shown that legitimate compliments are almost as good as pay raises to employees. This applies to people you encounter in other parts of life too. If a waiter does a good job, then in addition to a good tip, tell them they did a good job. And tell their manager the waiter did a good job, too.

Be a person who recognizes other people for what they do!

Day 37

"Every failure brings with it the seed of an equivalent success."

—Napoleon Hill

I have consistently told my oldest grandson to always benefit from his mistakes in life. Every mistake carries with it a lesson. The lesson is not just what not to do but also *how* not to do something or how to do it better or differently. These seeds of information are often lost as people are stressed by guilt or fear over their mistakes rather than analyzing them to see what they did and how not to do it again.

Science uses a system called trial and error in some experiments. This system depends on keeping notes on what was done, why it failed, and what to do differently next time. We need to do the same with our mistakes.

I tell people that anyone who says they have never made a mistake is either a liar or they are deluding themselves!

Day 38

"It is your responsibility to make sure that positive emotions constitute the dominating influence of your mind."

—Napoleon Hill

I cannot control how you feel, and you cannot control how I feel. I know you are thinking, "You can affect my feelings." Well, only if you let me! Like the quote says, you are responsible for your feelings.

If I call you a name, how you react is your responsibility. If you allow negative feelings to dominate your thoughts, then that is going to be how you react the majority of the time, even in good times. But if you practice positive thoughts, then you have a higher probability of reacting with a positive emotion even in a negative situation!

Regardless of whom, what, when, or where, *you* are ultimately the sole person responsible for how you react emotionally at any given time. *You* are responsible for maintaining positive emotions at all times. Easier said than done, yes. But it is good to practice, practice, practice!

Part I: Days 1–100

Day 39

"When you have eliminated all which is impossible, then whatever remains, however improbable, must be the truth."

—Arthur Conan Doyle

Many people will argue that this is not true. But if you read it slowly and think about what Doyle said, there is no other choice but what he says! Because what he says is true, good detectives and scientists—which are professions that employ similar skills—follow this idea.

My wife watches a lot of true crime shows on television, and with the advent of DNA evidence, there are many crimes where the idea expressed in today's quote creates some really unusual endings. One show featured the murder of a person that had gone unsolved for years, and there were several very viable suspects, but DNA evidence cleared them all. Finally, after decades of searching DNA records, the most improbable suspect was located and arrested. Without eliminating all the impossible and accepting the improbable, the murderer would never have been found.

When you are pursuing your dream, you might have to accept the rule expressed in today's quote to achieve your goal!

Day 40

"You cannot control the behavior of others, but you can always choose how you respond to it."

—Roy T. Bennett

Boy, is this fact! People are so unpredictable—family, friends, co-workers, etc. You never know how they are going to act or react. But no matter how they behave, you can control how you respond to their behavior. Even when they catch you completely off guard, if you have practiced positive thinking and emotional control, you can step back, take time to evaluate the situation, and approach it in a calm, cool, and positive manner.

People are a bundle of nerves and emotions and are reacting to input that you might not be aware of. The person going off on you might have just received terrible news, just had an argument, or be bipolar and not have had their medications. You can't assume it is you they are fired up about. If you do, you can accidentally cause long-term damage to your relationship.

It is best to be silent, and think, and allow the other person time to decompress before you respond. And maybe if you act like they haven't blown up, they will calm down. As the old saying goes, discretion is the better part of valor.

Day 41

> "The Chinese use two brushstrokes to write the word 'crisis.' One brush stroke stands for danger, the other for opportunity. In a crisis, be aware of the danger but recognize the opportunity."
>
> —John F. Kennedy

When the stock market crashed in 1929, and the great depression hit, people lost their fortunes, and people committed suicide as they saw their fortunes melt away. But at the same time, great fortunes were made as wise and wealthy investors bought the viable stocks at rock bottom prices and waited, knowing that in time, the market would recover. Historically, if you look at the stock market, for every dip, there is a rise and vice versa. The wise investor knows the old adage "buy low, sell high." The great depression was just a giant low!

In 2007–2008, the housing market crash led to a similar situation in real estate and somewhat in the overall stock market. I had a Thrift Savings Plan (which is like a 401K), and just as the market started to dip, I borrowed a large sum from my account to buy a house that was way below market value. Two years later, I sold the house for a large profit as prices went up, and I paid off my loan just as the market started recovering. I ended up making money during the recession. There's always opportunity in a crisis!

Day 42

"Start each day with a positive thought and a grateful heart."

—Roy T. Bennett

Hopefully, by now, thinking positive thoughts is becoming a habit for you. It is normal to develop a new habit in six weeks (or forty-two days), and this is day forty-two! You should be waking up in a positive way, looking forward to the new day and new opportunities, and being grateful for what you have. How can we expect to receive more if we do not appreciate what we already have?

Being positive and grateful allows you to see the world in a light that shows you the good side of things. You aren't bitter and jealous. Instead, you are happy with your life and happy for others, and that frees you to not only give of yourself but to receive graciously. The hardest thing for most people is to receive from others.

I know that when I started opening up and giving more to other people, I saw how hard it is for people to accept gifts. They want to pay you, or they feel obligated for what you offer, and so they often turn down something they truly need. Pride raises its ugly head and blocks them from receiving a blessing. Be open and grateful and accept what is there for you!

Day 43

> "Even if you are on the right track, you'll get run over if you just sit there."
>
> —Will Rogers

As I have mentioned on other days in this book, there is more to life than a dream; life requires action—*positive* action. The Bible says that "Faith without acts is dead." Simply put, you can believe, but you must put your belief into action. Regardless of what it is, you have to respond in a positive way.

On Day 24, I talked about the inventions I came up with decades ago but just put in a drawer, only to see someone else create them and sell them years later. Those people took action while I just sat there and got run over. I was on the right track, but I just sat there!

Don't let your dreams be a fatality. Get up and take action—*positive* action—to make them become a reality!

Day 44

> "It's not the size of the dog in the fight; it's the size of the fight in the dog."
>
> —Mark Twain

Ever watch a Chihuahua? It is one of the smallest dogs around, but it will attack a Great Dane and chase it down the street. The Great Dane could wipe a Chihuahua out, but the big dog only sees the big attitude in the little dog, and he runs from it. The Chihuahua thinks it is big and bad, so it goes after any and all targets!

I know people who are like that. My *wife* is like that. Don't mess with people who are like that! When they decide they can do something, you can't stop them.

That's how you have to be about your dream! I don't care who you are and what you have going for you, when it comes to your dream, you are a giant with all the assets in the world at your disposal. Go for it! Be a Chihuahua!

Part I: Days 1–100

Day 45

"Whatever you can do or dream you can, begin it. Boldness has genius, power, and magic in it!"

—Johann Wolfgang von Goethe

I woke up one morning and felt like I was supposed to write this book. I sat down and started putting it together and planning the printing and publishing. I researched places to get it done from the first words I put into the computer. I saved information, I studied books I had on my bookshelf, I dedicated time every day to writing and research, I told my wife I was doing it, and I told her she was my proofreader.

I planned the financing and distribution of the book as well as potential advertising and other means to sell it. I prayed about it, I thought about it much of my time, and I woke up thinking about it. And now, you are holding my dreams, my thoughts, my time, and my positive actions in your hands. Now, use it to take your dreams and create a reality of your own!

Day 46

"If you make a mistake and do not correct it, this is called a mistake."

—Confucius

We often think if we make a mistake, we should just move on and forget it. But that isn't right. We need to correct our mistakes and learn from them. Our mistakes are a stumbling block and a sign to other people of sloppy work on our part. We need to clean up our messes first and *then* move on.

This idea also extends to actions that would be mistakes if we didn't do them. At the market, if we get an item and then decide we don't want it, we don't dump it on the wrong shelf (especially perishables). Instead, we put it back where we got it. And when we load our groceries into a vehicle, we don't leave the cart in the parking lot. Instead, we take it to the cart rack or back to the store. We are positive and correct in our actions. We are people of excellence. If we can't be people of excellence, then we won't be excellent in our dreams!

Practice excellence and correct mistakes. If you do, you will find your life being more positive and fruitful!

Day 47

"Why are you trying so hard to fit in when you're born to stand out."

—Oliver James

We are people of unique and special character and excellence. We are not here to fit in; we are here to stand out! We are here to set the example and to lead by example. We display positive attitudes and show others how to live grateful, positive lives.

While other people are trying to conform to the group, we are setting the standard and developing new ideas and technologies. But do not look down on them. Be humble, and do not lower your standards to try to be accepted.

Positive people are looked at with suspicion by the negative world. But in reality, those in the negative world are jealous of your confidence. They are in fear, and they want to be reassured that things are okay.

Follow your dream and depend on your realistic view of the world to guide you at all times.

Day 48

> "If you change the way you look at things, the things you look at change."
>
> —Wayne W. Dyer

You've heard it here before: your attitude changes your world. How you see the world is how you react to it. If you are negative, then things you encounter will be negative. If you are positive, then things will have a positive outlook.

Let's say it starts to rain. Negative: "Oh no, it's raining, my day is ruined. I just washed my car; what a waste of time. I'm going to get wet, my plans are ruined, and my shoes will get muddy." Positive: "The grass and plants need this rain, and the air will be cleaner afterward. I love the smell of rain. I think I'll stay inside and read today."

Simple positive ideas make the difference. You encounter someone you've been having an issue with? Maybe use that time to get to know them better. Maybe you can resolve your issues and understand the other person better. Maybe you can even become friends!

Day 49

"Aim higher in case you fall short."

—Suzanne Collins

I used to teach classes to new employees, and in one of the classes, I talked about setting goals. Today's quote was one of the points I always emphasized. I told the employees that when they set goals, they need three levels of goals: short-term, midterm, and long-term.

Short-term goals would be ones you could readily achieve and would be done daily. These would also be reinforcing as they would provide quick feedback and personal satisfaction. Midterm goals would be an accumulation of the short-term goals plus some higher-level achievable goals that would motivate them further. And long-term goals would be goals for lifestyle improvements, like college degrees, job promotions, buying a house, etc.

I also told the new employees to set a long-term "reach for the stars" goal. This would be something they imagined they couldn't presently do but that, in time, they might see they were actually in a position to accomplish. That way, even if they fell short, they would reach higher than they could imagine! For some of them, the "reach for the stars" goal was the goal of owning a luxury car. A few years later, some of the employees came to me and told me they already had their luxury car and felt they should have aimed higher. They were now setting even higher dream targets!

Day 50

"We either make ourselves miserable, or we make ourselves strong. The amount of work is the same."

—Carlos Castaneda

So true! Sometimes, as I watch people, I think they actually work *harder* to make themselves miserable. They spend so much time dreading tasks that when it comes time to actually do the tasks, these people are already worn out mentally. These people only see the worst in other people and fuss about every little thing that comes along.

The thing I never understood was that people like that would avoid working and do nothing but then complain that time was dragging at work. I would work at anything I could to make time go faster! Some people never seem to grasp the idea that staying busy keeps them from paying attention to the clock and other people's business.

The people I'm talking about dreaded coming to work and started dreading the next day before they even finished the day they were on. I often wondered if they sat at home complaining about having to go to work. Why not use that time to make yourself stronger?

Day 51

"At the end of the day, let there be no excuses, no explanations, and no regrets."

—Steve Maraboli

If you put in a full day and get everything done that you can, you don't have to worry about this issue. It's only when you have goofed off or avoided something that you have to make excuses or give explanations or have regrets. I've certainly been there, done that, and have the T-shirt. But I also know the satisfaction of a completed day with no bad feelings, which is much more desirable.

On Day 6, I talked about making a list at the beginning of the day. Well, doing that really helps you reach the end of the day with a sense of completion and satisfaction. Give your dreams the best you have, and rest easy knowing you are making positive progress every day.

Day 52

"If you dare nothing, then when the day is over, nothing is all you will have gained."

—Neil Gaiman

So many people are afraid of taking a risk by going beyond their comfort zone that they never try! If you stay in your comfort zone, then you'll never achieve your dreams.

The Wright brothers had a bicycle shop, but they dreamed of flying. They had to go beyond their comfort zone to develop a flying machine. They risked a lot, they dared a lot, and they created a machine that could fly. It might not seem like much today, but back then, it was an amazing feat.

There was a song at the turn of the century that had the words, "Those magnificent men in their flying machines . . ." in reference to the Wright brothers' invention of the airplane. Imagine what daring it took for the brothers to be the very first. Sometimes, it takes daring to be magnificent!

Day 53

"If you hang out with chickens, you're going to cluck, and if you hang out with eagles, you're going to fly."

—Steve Maraboli

It *does* matter who you hang out with. I once had a great mentor advise me that if you want to get better at something, find someone who has already excelled at that thing and hang out with them. There is no sense in reinventing the wheel. Instead, learn how someone successful did it and follow their lead. You can improve on it, but you don't need to reinvent it!

When I started playing golf, I played with people of the same skill level I played at, and my game did not improve. When I moved to Texas, I fell in with a crowd that played much better than I did. They didn't mind me playing along with them, and I wasn't intimidated by them, and in a short time, my game improved dramatically! Usually, the better crowd is also less likely to be naysayers since they have already progressed and have a more positive attitude.

Turkeys flock together; eagles fly alone!

Day 54

"The surest way to make your dreams come true is to live them."

—Roy T. Bennett

I am going to use another golf analogy to illustrate this. It might not be the best analogy, but it shows how I helped myself achieve a dream.

At one time in my life, I had a dream of becoming a scratch golfer (which means shooting par). At that time, I was actually shooting about twelve to fifteen strokes over par on average and playing with people about the same skill level as me. I read an article by a man in Washington state about visualizing and playing as if you were in a tournament, and I decided to try it with a slight twist. I decided to tell myself I was a scratch golfer, and on every shot, I told myself what the outcome was going to be in advance and visualized the shot before I hit it.

I did that for several months, and soon, I was playing scratch golf. In one six-week period, I played in four states on six different courses, and the highest score I shot was par. I was living my dream. Unfortunately, other things in life interfered, and soon, I stopped playing entirely, having decided that supporting my family was more important than golf. But for a moment in time, I had accomplished a dream.

You can live your dream, too. And if your dream is important enough to dedicate your life to, you can make it real. And by the way, I have no regrets about giving golf up at that time. It was fun while it lasted.

Part I: Days 1–100

Day 55

"Dripping water hollows out stone, not through force but through persistence."

—Ovid

I have seen, and probably you have too, some amazing things in nature. I have seen a palm root shoot up a sprout that cracked a concrete foundation and then push up a little green shoot that was soft and supple. I have seen roots destroy concrete foundations and driveways. And I have seen flowers growing up through concrete. The idea of dripping water hollowing stone is minor in comparison, and all of this is from perseverance! Slow and steady wins the race is an old saying but a true one.

The secret to success is perseverance. Just keep plugging away and never give up. When you watch the Olympics, you aren't seeing people who a few weeks ago decided to become runners or gymnasts or shot-putters. Instead, you are watching people who started years ago—decades in some cases—and have trained and persevered until the day you see them. They do all that for one brief moment in time.

Your pursuit of your dream will be the same. It will be a marathon of pursuit so that one day the world will incorrectly say, "Boy were they lucky!"

Day 56

"Though nobody can go back and make a new beginning, anyone can start over and make a new ending."

—Chico Xavier

I read the story of Harlan Sanders, the founder of Kentucky Fried Chicken. To me, it was an amazing and inspiring story because it is the story of a man who never gave up. Regardless of how many unsuccessful ventures he had, he kept trying, and age did not lessen his desire to succeed. I strongly suggest you look him up and read the true story; it is intricate and will surprise you.

In short, after many trials and bad business adventures, Sanders tried the one thing he was really good at, and that was frying chicken. And with that, at age sixty-five, he became a success. The rest is history—*delicious* history.

Sanders wrote his new ending at sixty-five. Grandma Moses wrote her new ending even later. In her eighties, she became a well-known artist!

Your past doesn't define you, and it doesn't limit you. You aren't over until you quit! As the famous philosopher Yogi Berra once said, "It ain't over 'til it's over."

Day 57

"Life has no remote. Get up and change it yourself!"

—Mark A. Cooper

I was once involved in a homeless ministry in the Atlanta area. It was a yearlong program of multiple classes and smaller programs designed to allow an individual to change their perspectives and learn a trade or profession and get an education. Through doing so, they could save money and reenter life as a taxpaying, working member of society with an apartment and possibly a vehicle. Many of them did, but there were those who dropped out, saying the program didn't work and was a waste of their time. The truth is that the dropouts didn't work at it hard enough or long enough to know. As today's quote alludes to, they expected someone else to do it by remote control instead of them getting off their butts and doing it themselves.

    I used to say that there are some people who could be starving to death, and you could send them to a buffet restaurant, and they would come out hungry and say there was nothing there to eat, while others would gorge themselves on everything there. Opportunity is everywhere, but you have to reach out and grab it for yourself!

Day 58

"He that can have patience can have what he will."

—Benjamin Franklin

Patience is a virtue, and most of us lack virtue! The problem with most people is that we live in a fast-food society, and we have a fast-food mentality. We want it *now*. I saw a little blurb in *Reader's Digest* that wrapped this concept up in a nutshell. It said, "Lord, give me patience, and give it to me right now!"

Anything worth having is worth waiting for, and your dreams will take time and patience to develop to perfection. Some dreams will take longer than others. Part of developing a positive attitude is developing patience and perseverance.

Patience, Grasshopper!

Part I: Days 1–100

Day 59

"Strong people have a strong sense of self-worth and self-awareness; they don't need the approval of others."

—Roy T. Bennett

If you need the approval of others, then you are a prisoner of their approval. They can control you and what you do. You will limit your actions to what *they* approve, and you will operate only in *their* scope of what is acceptable. Your dreams will belong to them and will not be yours.

You are unique and special and do not need anyone's approval. I am not telling you to go forth arrogantly and violate the law. But do not limit yourself to what others approve. Seek your dreams according to what *you* know is right and according to *your* purpose in life.

Columbus set sail for the new world. Despite what all the wise men said about the new world not existing, he had a dream and a purpose, and he found the passage to America. Lewis and Clark explored the new territory and found the passage to the Pacific Ocean. So, be bold and trust your instincts!

Day 60

"Once we accept our limits, we can go beyond them."

—Albert Einstein

Notice that today's quote says our *limits*, not our limitations; there is a difference. Any athlete training for their event has to find their own personal limits and then push themselves beyond those limits to achieve their best.

Decades ago, people believed it was impossible to break the four-minute mile. But then, Roger Bannister pushed himself beyond his limits, and one day, he broke the four-minute "limit" and ran the mile in *less* than four minutes. Once he had done it, in the next few weeks, several more runners did it, too! Knowing it could be done, they were psychologically able to achieve the feat as well.

Find your limit in your chosen area, and then find a way to surpass that limit. Once you do, you can reach new and amazing heights for your dreams. Tiger Woods showed professional golf a new standard in golf performance, and in a few years, other golfers started performing at his level. At first, people thought Tiger had lost some of his talent, but the truth was, he had simply motivated others to reach his level!

Limits are meant to be broken. Break yours!

Day 61

"Don't think. Thinking is the enemy of creativity. It's self-conscious, and anything self-conscious is lousy. You can't 'try' to do things. You simply 'must' do things."

—Ray Bradbury

This quote might sound contradictory to what I have been espousing but read it again and recognize what Mr. Bradbury is really saying. He is telling us not to get in our own way by overanalyzing (or "paralysis by analysis"). Many great things come from instinctive reasoning rather than hard thought. Our subconscious sees and recognizes things quicker and better than our conscious. If you have a "hunch," listen to it, and give it a try! That "gut feeling" might be the answer you are looking for.

It is easy to talk yourself out of the right answer, especially if you are educated in a field. Traditional learning says something is not so, but the gut feeling says try it. You rationalize that it just isn't right, and so you don't try your gut feeling, and you end up missing out on the unique solution.

Just try your hunch. The old fuddy-duddies probably don't know the answer themselves anyway! Much of our great discovery has been accidental or from trying something that wasn't according to science. Penicillin was the result of sloppy practice.

It's *your* dream, so use *your* instincts!

Day 62

"Difficulties strengthen the mind, as labor does the body."

—Lucius Annaeus Seneca

It is how you handle a difficulty that determines the outcome and how you come out of it. Many people face difficulties and come out discouraged, broken, and defeated, while others come out stronger, ready to face life more determined to succeed. It's all in your attitude!

Life will throw problems at you. How will you handle them? The best way to be prepared is to realize that . . . there *will* be problems! Don't walk around with your head in the sand, hoping nothing will happen. Instead, live what I call a defensive lifestyle: be prepared for problems, live with a positive outlook, but be ready for the negative.

If you are pursuing your dream, know what can go wrong and be ready if it does. Don't let it destroy your dream. Instead, learn from it and move forward after you overcome it. Sometimes, what appears to be the worst situation is actually your greatest steppingstone forward. I talked about Steve Jobs getting fired from his own company, and because of that, he had time and motivation to create the iPhone, which became his and Apple's greatest asset. And it put Steve Jobs back in control of Apple again!

Use your difficulties to strengthen yourself!

Part I: Days 1–100

Day 63

"So many things are possible as long as you don't know they are impossible."

—Mildred D. Taylor

The bumblebee doesn't know it cannot fly, so it does it anyway! Ignore the experts when they say it is impossible.

In the nineteenth century, they said men couldn't travel over twenty-five miles an hour because they could not breathe at speeds greater than that. And they said women couldn't travel at speeds over thirty-five miles an hour because if they did and had to stop suddenly, their uteruses would fly out of their bodies. In the nineteenth century, the head of the US Patent Office said they should close the office because all that could be invented had already been invented. And before the Wright brothers invented the airplane, it was said that humans would never be able to fly.

What can *you* do that experts say is impossible? To find out, ignore the experts! I had a friend who used to say that the definition of experts is: "Ex" = has been, and "Spurt" = drip under pressure. His meaning was that many so-called experts know absolutely nothing!

Day 64

"What is now proved was once only imagined."

—William Blake

So *very* true! Flight was once—only just over a hundred years ago at the time of this writing—an imagination. Now, anyone can buy a ticket and fly anywhere in the world in a few hours, in luxury. And the smartphone was a fantasy, but now, even people in Third World countries can talk and video-call with people on opposite sides of the world. Space flight was the thing of science fiction just sixty-plus years ago, but now, we have walked on the moon, and people live in space, on space stations.

Daily, we use technology that less than a lifetime ago was undreamed of. I am typing up this book on a machine we didn't imagine possible in my teen years! So, what can *you* create in your dreams that tomorrow will be routine?

Part I: Days 1–100

Day 65

"The most important decision you make is to be in a good mood."

—Voltaire

Oh my gosh, how true! It has taken me so long to learn this. I have let myself drift into bad moods for no reason and ruined great days for me and the people I love for no reason. So instead, wake up and *decide* you are going to be in a good mood!

You can either be in a good mood or a bad mood, and it takes the same effort either way. But life is so much better if you decide on the good mood. Don't let clowns ruin your day. Look at the world in a good mood—see the positive, the humor, and the best parts. It is easy if you practice it.

Will you have interruptions? Yes! But all you have to do is self-correct and get back on course. It's as easy to go back to a good mood as it is to go into a bad mood, so make the right choice. Life is so much better in the good lane.

I always used to wonder how Mr. Rogers stayed so upbeat. And then I figured it out: he made the right choice every day. You can, too!

Day 66

"You're never given a dream without also being given the power to make it true."

—Richard Bach

The ability to make your dream come true is your ability to pursue it with all your might, to realistically and enthusiastically seek it with persistence and perseverance, and to ignore the naysayers and believe in yourself and the dream and prepare yourself for a life of adventure. No one says it will be easy, but it will be exciting, and it will be rewarding.

Dreams are not unrealistic fantasies; they are achievable realities that might require stretching beyond what the average person's limitations are. You can't be average and achieve your dream. You have to be extraordinary and ignore the established boundaries. Trust your instincts, seek others with vision, think outside the box, and reach for the stars. You have been blessed with a unique dream and purpose in life. Go for it and achieve it. You and you alone are capable!

Day 67

"Always bear in mind that your own resolution to succeed is more important than anything."

—Abraham Lincoln

No one in this world can make up your mind or resolve for you to accomplish your dream. You alone can do that, and your resolution is the most important thing in the world. If you are not 100 percent committed, then no one can drag you across the finish line. If you *are* 100 percent committed, then no one can stop you from finishing!

Make up your mind: either be all in or not in. The success of your mission is contingent on your commitment, and if you are involving others, their success is contingent on your commitment too!

Day 68

"Things do not change; we change."

—Henry David Thoreau

Absolute truth! If you get up in the morning, walk outside, and look at the scene outside your doorway, and it is unappealing because you don't like the colors, then there's not much you can do. The next morning, if you decide you will like the colors, and you walk outside, and now you like the scene because you have changed your opinion, then nothing outside has changed, but *you* have!

Your world can remain the same, but you can change to accommodate the world, and, in doing so, your outlook will change. The gloomy can become cheerful and the depressing happy . . . *if* you change. As stated earlier in this book, it's not what we look at but rather what we see that matters.

If you can't change your world, then change yourself!

Part I: Days 1–100

Day 69

"Our life is what our thoughts make it."

—Marcus Aurelius

Here's that same point again. We make our life and our world what it is by what we think—by our attitude. I see this every day in almost every person I deal with. People approach situations with dread and negative feelings and make their own lives miserable when all they have to do to make their lives happy is change how they think!

Instead of dreading their jobs, people can look forward to them by seeing them as rewarding and good rather than mundane and depressing. Think about other people in positive ways, too, rather than as bothersome and a hindrance. Look for the bright side of life instead of the woe is me side.

If you always look on the gloomy side of life, then your life will be miserable. But if you instead look on the positive side, your life will be positive. Your life is what you make it. It's just as easy to be in a good mood as in a bad one. But it's a lot more fun in a good mood!

Day 70

"A goal without a plan is just a wish."
—Antoine de Saint-Exupéry

When you have a dream, you have to set a goal to accomplish it. When you set a goal, you need to establish a plan to accomplish that goal. The best way to establish that plan is to write it out, review it, refine it, and set a time frame to go after it. Without a written, logical plan, you don't have a start point and check points to follow.

You don't have to stay with your original plan all the way along toward your goal. You will, of necessity, modify the plan as you go. But you need it to start out and to guide you along your path. Your plan is like a map to follow on a trip; you have to know where you are at the beginning, where you are going, and the trail you have to follow. You should list your preparations, the steps to follow, and the assets and people you think you will need.

Once you start putting your plan into action, you will modify it as you progress, but you will always have a guide. Without the plan, you just have a fantasy and will probably never get started. So, write the plan!

Day 71

"Always dream and shoot higher than you know you can do. Do not bother just to be better than your contemporaries or predecessors. Try to be better than yourself."

—William Faulkner

Don't compare yourself to others. They aren't you, and they don't have your dream. You are unique, and your dream is unique.

First off, always aim for the stars. That way, if you fall short, you will still be way above everybody else. Secondly, there is no one you can compare to. *You* are one of a kind!

It's easy to hit a low mark, and you will then quit because you think you succeeded. But instead, try aiming high, and if you miss, try again. Keep aiming high until you achieve success!

Never compare yourself to others. You are unique and special, and there's no one to compare yourself to. Let *them* compare themselves to *you*! Meantime, focus on your dream and let the rest of the world blur out.

Day 72

"Too often, we underestimate the power of a touch, a smile, a kind word, a listening ear, an honest compliment, or the smallest act of caring, all of which have the potential to turn a life around."

—Leo Buscaglia

When you are working with others, and especially when they are working *for* you, remember to keep their feelings foremost in your mind. They aren't robots without feelings and emotions; they are people with feelings and cares. Remember to pay attention to what they do and what is going on in their lives.

Don't flatter the people you work with or lie to them. But when they do a good job, compliment them, and praise them in front of their peers. When they are tired and down, encourage them with a kind word. When they are having personal issues, empathize and give them time to handle their problems. They will remember it and give you their best. It will make you a better person, and regardless of how it affects your progress, you will feel better about your environment . . . as will they!

Day 73

"I must be willing to give up what I am in order to become what I will be."

—Albert Einstein

Sometimes—most of the time—in order to achieve your dream, you must change who or what you are. This is one of the hardest obstacles we face in the pursuit of our dreams. It means changing and giving up a part of our self-image or interests that we may not want to give up. We might be in a career that we love, but to achieve our dream, we have to give up that career. Or it might be a relationship or a friendship. We might have to relocate or drop out of school—something we really do not want to do!

Now, right in the middle of achieving our dreams and reaching our goals, we face a major decision that is a hurdle we never saw coming. What do we do? I can't give you the answer. But I can tell you that when this hurdle arises, you have a serious decision to make, and it might cause you second thoughts for years. It did for me, but in the end, I came out ok!

Day 74

"No matter how your heart is grieving, if you keep on believing, the dreams that you wish will come true."

—Walt Disney

Simple words from a song, but so very, very true! The key word or words are "keep on believing." You *must* believe. If your dream is real, and you know it is for you, then no matter what, just keep believing!

The power of positive thinking is connected to positive actions powered by positive and real belief that it will happen. That, together with a persistent effort, will allow you to succeed. You might suffer pain, you might grieve, and it will take time. But just keep believing, and one day, your dream will manifest and come true!

Day 75

"Two roads diverged in a wood, and I took the one less traveled by, and that has made all the difference."

—Robert Frost

Too often, we want to follow the herd and travel down the road everyone else does. Unfortunately, everyone else is failing or falling into negativity and lack of success. Sometimes, the best course is to take the lonely road that no one else is on.

There are fresh and untouched opportunities on the road less traveled—new views and new challenges. It's less crowded, and we will have an unfettered path to travel. Far from the maddening crowd, we can think clearly and move easily.

Don't pick a road just because everyone else is on it. Instead, pick the road that has the most opportunity!

Day 76

"The question is not what you look at but what you see."

—Henry David Thoreau

On Day 68, I mentioned that what you look at and what you see is not always the same thing. I look at the ocean and see a place to fish. My wife looks at the ocean, and she sees a place to lie in the sand and sunbathe. I look at the woods and see a place to hunt. My wife looks at the woods, and she sees a place full of ticks and bugs—a place to avoid! I look at a mall as a place to be bored all day. My wife looks at a mall as a place to shop and find the latest bargains.

We all look at something and see what we want to see. What do *you* see?

Day 77

"Lack of direction, not lack of time, is the problem. We all have twenty-four-hour days."

—Zig Ziglar

I love reading Zig Ziglar books. He was the greatest motivator and sales trainer I have ever read about. He was down to earth and a straight shooter. One of his favorite statements was talking about negative thinking as "stinking thinking."

Today's quote is *so* true. We all have the same amount of time in a day, but lack of direction, lack of planning, and lack of focus are our biggest problems. That's why early on in this book, I stressed making a list and following it to make sure you get things done during the day. The list gives you a sense of direction.

Later on in this book, we will talk more about finding a direction for your day. But for now, I suggest you get some of Zig's books and read them. They are informative and funny. He was a great man!

Day 78

"You see things, and you say, 'Why?' But I dream things that never were, and I say, 'Why not?'"

—George Bernard Shaw

Heck yeah! I love this statement. John F. Kennedy used a variation of this as well.

So many people are pessimistic. They see a glass as half empty, but I say it is half full. They say it can't be done, but I ask why not? Most people don't want you succeeding because it will make them look bad, but I want people to succeed because I want others to know it is possible!

We have airplanes today because the Wright brothers said, "Why not?" We have space flight because someone said, "Why not?" You have smartphones and computers because someone said, "Why not?" You are reading this book because I said, "Why not?"

What's *your* dream that we will share because *you* will say, "Why not?"

Day 79

"Believe in yourself. You are braver than you think, more talented than you know, and capable of more than you imagine."

—Roy T. Bennett

The saddest thing I have ever seen is a person with great potential who doesn't believe in themself. It is so frustrating to me and so sad to watch them fail just because they won't try or because they think they can't do it.

Years ago, while I lived in Texas, I played golf with a man who could routinely shoot scores well below par on any course we played. He had numerous people offer to sponsor him on the pro tour if . . . he would just try. But he refused to try for fear that he wasn't good enough! Sadly, he ended up running a driving range and then working in his wife's restaurant. Maybe he wouldn't have made it on tour, but he never tried! That is the sad part.

So many people have skills and talents that they never put to the test in life because they are afraid they will fail, while lesser-qualified people try and succeed! Just believe in yourself and give it a shot. What have you got to lose?

Day 80

"Do not go where the path may lead, go instead where there is no path and leave a trail."

—Ralph Waldo Emerson

Most people go to college and then take a job where they do what has already been proven and is easy. Or they come out of school and take up a trade that is easy and a tried-and-true profession, usually following in someone else's footsteps. Those people sometimes end up leading mundane lives, living in the same house in the same neighborhood most if not all their lives, and retiring late in life with minimal savings and no real memories.

A chosen few will find a path of adventure in out-of-the-norm professions or in creating a new path altogether and will establish a lifestyle few will understand. These people will live lives they love and may never retire, but if they do, they will have memories that few can compare to. These lives might be lives you read about or lives you never hear about, but they are special and unique.

Don't settle for the mundane and easy path. Break new ground and live your life with gusto!

Day 81

"Talent hits a target no one else can hit. Genius hits a target no one else can see."

—Arthur Schopenhauer

Nikola Tesla had visions that still, today, baffle even the greatest minds. Some of his ideas were so far ahead of his time that we haven't caught up to them in reality. Unfortunately, his notes disappeared after his death, so we will probably never know all he was working on. But what we are aware of is mind-boggling. The basic concept of the smartphone was described by Tesla as far back as the 1920s, and the motor used in today's Tesla automobiles is essentially one he designed almost ninety years ago.

A real genius is capable of visualizing things the average mind can't even conceive. In his book *Think and Grow Rich,* Napoleon Hill talks about some of the great industrialists of the nineteenth century and early twentieth century. These men conceived ideas and businesses that moved the world forward exponentially and did it in short periods. They were geniuses in their respective fields.

Today, we are privileged to be witnesses to other great geniuses like Jobs, Gates, Bezos, Musk . . . all of whom are moving us ahead in leaps and bounds into a technological future. Sit back, watch, enjoy, and learn from them. But be sure to *use* what you learn!

Day 82

"Pain is inevitable. Suffering is optional."

—Haruki Murakami

What happens to you can affect you in many ways. What I want you to remember from today's quote is simple. You can control the effect!

Failure can be devastating, or it can be instructional. It is your choice. Loss can be disastrous or motivational. It is your choice.

Whatever you encounter, *you* can decide how you react to it. It is *your* choice! (Think about it.)

Part I: Days 1–100

Day 83

"I have not failed. I've just found 10,000 ways that won't work."

—Thomas A. Edison

Failure is always a lesson learned—a lesson on what doesn't work and a path not to take. The failure might be a nano-step from success or a mile off target. The only way to find out is to try again with a change in your approach.

Sometimes, failure will produce a success in something else that you weren't expecting! Many products we have today were created as a result of the failure of experiments to create something else. Sticky notes came about as a result of trying to create glue that didn't stick to items permanently. The glue that was invented wasn't what the inventors wanted but was later used on paper used for notes. Later, the paper was marketed as sticky notes. The glue was an accident.

Learn from failure and know that it is not a waste of time and effort!

Day 84

"There are only two ways to live your life. One is as though nothing is a miracle. The other is as though everything is a miracle."

—Albert Einstein

How you look at life is the key to your world! People like Einstein look at life and see the miracles in everyday things that we sometimes take for granted. Seeing these tiny miracles in life's daily activities can and will trigger ideas that lead to great ideas and creations. Understanding "why" is what drives geniuses, and the simplest things in life are the key to the secrets of the universe.

When oil fields in Ohio first started producing in the 1800s, most people saw just the crude petroleum. But John D. Rockefeller saw potential in the refining of that petroleum. He set about to develop a system to refine the kerosene and refine it in its purest form. Once he achieved it, he then set a standard of purity for the nation and called it "Standard Oil." Then, he marketed it and set up a distribution system, and quickly, he became one of the richest men in America. He saw the miracle in refining the oil coming out of the ground, and he used it to become a mega-millionaire!

Day 85

"Do it now!"

—Napoleon Hill

Procrastination has destroyed more great ideas and people than anything in history. If you have a dream or an idea and you know it is worth the effort, don't hesitate. Go after it *NOW*!

You might not think you are ready to go after your dream or idea, but in reality, you will *never* be ready. You have to just go for it. Any start is better than just sitting there doing nothing. You will find that action creates action. You will make mistakes, but you will learn from them.

Amazon started in a garage! Jeff Bezos had an idea, and he went for it. He didn't wait until he could rent a warehouse and set up a big delivery system. He started with what he had, where he was. I wonder how many well-intentioned people told him he was crazy. Ha, ha, ha!

Day 86

"Begin anywhere."

—John Cage

Like we discussed yesterday, Jeff Bezos started Amazon in his garage. Bill Gates started Microsoft in a garage, too. Where did Steve Jobs start Apple? In his garage. It seems like garages are the great beginning place!

Famous Amos cookies were baked in a small kitchen, and Amos went door to door with them and even handed them out free on the streets. Harlan Sanders of Kentucky Fried Chicken started selling his fried chicken in a small diner and then went local, then regional, etc. Start where you are, and then grow! Ray Kroc had an idea and bought a few small burger joints. They were called . . . McDonald's!

Start wherever *you* are!

Day 87

"If you are ready for the secret, you already possess one half of it. Therefore, you will readily recognize the other half the moment it reaches your mind."

—Napoleon Hill

You have to be ready for your dream and how it will come about. Most of the people that have built their dreams did not have any idea how the dream would actually pan out; they just knew they had a dream, and they believed it would happen. They went for it, and somewhere along the way, the pieces started coming together. They saw the pieces fitting together and recognized them because they saw the big picture and saw where the pieces fit.

Andrew Carnegie was involved in iron but knew that iron was not the future. He knew that steel was the answer but knew that the conventional way to make steel was not the answer. When he saw the Bessemer process, he immediately recognized it as the answer because he had the dream and the Bessemer process fit the dream. He immediately outfitted his factories with the Bessemer process, and soon, Carnegie was the richest man in the world.

If you have the dream, you will recognize the components to complete the dream!

Day 88

"The cause of poverty is traceable directly to the worldwide habit of trying to reap without sowing."

—Unknown

The Bible says you will reap what you sow. Greed tries to reap without sowing, but soon, there is nothing but barren fields. Soon, there is famine, drought, and poverty over the land. You cannot have prosperity and success in your dreams if you don't sow as you go!

Sow by lifting up others, including others in your dreams. Put back into the community. Give to the church or to charity, help others with their dreams, and pay your workers well. Greed doesn't have a place in your dreams. Frugality is good, but don't confuse greed and frugality.

Day 89

"Faith removes limitations!"

—Napoleon Hill

I constantly emphasize "belief"—believing in yourself, believing in your dreams. Faith is belief. If you have faith, you can do all things!

Understanding that it takes time and faith will stand in good stead in achieving your dreams. The time will vary from person to person. So, never judge your dream's fruition against someone else's. If your dream is being achieved faster, don't get big-headed. If yours is slower, don't get depressed. Each dream has a growth cycle of its own.

Corn grows in a few months, but the giant bamboo tree takes five years. Have faith and wait for your dream!

Day 90

"Every man is what he is because of the dominating thoughts which he permits to occupy his mind."

—Napoleon Hill

Amen! That quote is really all that needs to be said!

A serial killer thinks only about killing. A compulsive gambler thinks only about gambling. A drug addict thinks about their next fix. A successful person thinks positive thoughts!

What do *you* think about most?

Day 91

"You have nothing to start with, except the capacity to know what you want and the determination to stand by that desire until you realize it."

—Napoleon Hill

The basic tools of success! Without these, you cannot go anywhere, but with them, you can go anywhere. It's all up to you and your determination!

So many people, especially today, are aimless in life. They have no goals, no plans, and no determination to accomplish anything. Many don't even show up to work on a regular basis. Your competition in the workforce is dwindling. Your competition in accomplishing greatness is almost none!

But don't let that lull you into complacency. Instead, use it to fuel you to rocket ahead even faster. You have an open field ahead of you!

Day 92

"One sound idea is all that one needs to achieve success."

—Napoleon Hill

Ideas like this:

- Harlan Sanders had fried chicken.
- Ray Kroc had hamburger franchises.
- Jeff Bezos has online retailing.
- Zuckerberg has social media.
- Elon Musk has electric automobiles.
- Steve Jobs had computers.
- Bill Gates has computer programs.
- John Rockefeller had refining kerosene.
- Andrew Carnegie had steel.
- Famous Amos has chocolate chip cookies.

What do *you* have?

Day 93

"Desire backed by faith knows no such word as impossible."

—Napoleon Hill

Let your dreams become obsessions, and let your desires become stronger than any excuses not to succeed. Believe in your ability to accomplish your dreams and desires and go for them with all you have.

People like Rockefeller and Carnegie pursued their dreams passionately and unwaveringly. They envisioned their dreams completed before they were actually completed, and they raced toward their dreams to embrace them. Pursue your dreams the same way: see them as already real and run to embrace them.

Desire and faith are the building blocks and cement of your reality. Use them to create your future!

Day 94

"In the end, it's not the years in your life that count. It's the life in your years."

—Abraham Lincoln

You can live a hundred years and accomplish nothing of value, or you can live twenty years and impact the world. I recently read that many of the founding fathers of this nation were active and impacting the nation's future in their teens and early twenties, and most before they were in their forties. It seems you read about people living to be in their nineties or even their hundreds, but you often don't read about what they have accomplished beyond that feat.

It's not unusual for older people to have an impact. Benjamin Franklin was older, and many modern people of note have been in their later years before they had major impacts. But for the most part, the people really impacting the world seem to be doing so in their early years. Maybe if we don't get started doing something early, we get complacent—satisfied with the status quo—and settle into a rut?

Exam your life. If you are still young, get a vision and get started. If you are older, get a renewed vision and get started again. It's never too late, and it's exciting to start a new venture!

Part I: Days 1–100

Day 95

"A man without ambition is like a beautiful caterpillar—it can creep, but it cannot fly."

—Henry Ward Beecher

Like I said on Days 24 and 26, it is a sad thing when a person has talent or intelligence but no ambition. I will now say in expansion of that notion that anyone—regardless of talent or intelligence—without ambition is a sad person.

I worked with a homeless ministry for some time, and I often heard people say that their present situation was because of where they came from or where they grew up, and many because they only had one parent. It turned out that most of them had it better growing up than I did but—putting aside mental health or substance abuse problems—maybe lacked the ambition to try anything and never achieved anything. Sometimes, I would talk about my past, and they would say things like, "But you . . . ." And I would stop them and say, "No, the difference is that I did something about it." They didn't like that, but my point was to encourage them that it wasn't too late. Some took heed and tried new opportunities, and some did lift themselves out of their situation, but most did not.

You *must* find ambition!

Day 96

"Be a king in your dreams. Make your vow that you will reach that position, with untarnished reputation, and make no other vow to distract your attention."

—Andrew Carnegie

Being the king is nothing more than being the one in charge. Don't take this in a sexist vein; you can be the queen if you would like. Just be the monarch of your life and your dream.

The monarch rules the show. They dictate the direction of movement, control the flow of assets, and control the action. As the monarch's "kingdom" grows, so too the power and influence grow and thereby their reputation as respectable. And others will honor that reputation.

Maintain the good reputation you build by doing things with integrity and treating those with whom you deal with the same respect you desire. Keep your word, and do not make other vows that will distract you from what your purpose is. In a nutshell, take responsibility for your dreams and for pursuing them with integrity and character!

Day 97

"The men who have succeeded are men who have chosen one line and stuck to it."

—Andrew Carnegie

The biggest mistake most people make initially is to try to succeed in too many areas at once. If you have noticed, the greatest successes tend to come from people who first focus on just one area. Bill Gates focused on programing. Steve Jobs focused on hardware. Jeff Bezos focused on online retailing. You rarely see someone successful start out doing multiple fields at once.

After someone succeeds at one thing, they might diversify. But they tend to focus on one thing at a time. You should, too! If your dream is in the stock market, don't try to be a doctor and a pro golfer and a sailor all at the same time. Focus on one thing at a time.

Day 98

"It's not what happens to you but how you react to it that matters."

—Epictetus

I presented this in part on an earlier day of this book, that what really matters in life is how you react to what impacts your life. Things happen, and you can't avoid that. But what you *can* avoid is letting them mess you up. An obstacle, failures, financial upsets, personal issues—all of these occur in life. But how you handle them determines how your life turns out.

I have seen people so devastated by a divorce that they let it ruin their lives and careers. One person I encountered in the homeless ministry I worked with was there because of a divorce that had caused him to give up a successful career in management and take to the streets. It was a waste of talent but his choice. Another person was a trained radiologist, but he got involved in drugs and lost his certification. Even after he got straight, he wouldn't go into another field. He just gave up and became homeless. It was a waste of education and intelligence but his choice.

Don't let life's stumbling blocks destroy you. When you get knocked down, get back up and regroup!

Day 99

"Any person capable of angering you becomes your master; he can anger you only when you permit yourself to be disturbed by him."

—Epictetus

This is so true! *You* are the one who allows another person to control your life. I've heard so many people say, "They make me so angry!" No, you allowed them to make you so angry.

If you know someone is going to push your buttons, then be ready to ignore them or don't allow them to get to you. Control yourself and get the upper hand. That is the best way to get to them! I know that is not always easy, but practice it mentally and be ready. You will be surprised how good it feels to be in control and not let someone else control you.

Day 100

"No pressure, no diamonds."
—Thomas Carlyle

I've heard that it takes both heat and extreme pressure for long periods to create a diamond. If you are going to become great, you must learn to operate under intense pressure. It is easy to do things when there is no pressure or stress, but when the pressure is on, you have to be able to think clearly, react to the situation, and be calm.

When I went through Officer Candidate School, the Tactical Officers harassed us constantly. Some of my fellow students cracked under the pressure and quit, and others complained about the harassment. I explained to them that the harassment was to teach us how to function under pressure. When we went into combat, it would really be bad, with enemy fire and people dying. So, I told my classmates to relax and be glad it was just people yelling at us. After that, most of them functioned better, understanding why the harassment existed.

Pressure serves a purpose. It makes you better!

PART II

~DAYS 101–200~

Day 101

"When the crowd is foolishly running blindly toward the cliff, it is the wise ones running away from the cliff who are thought to be foolish!"

—John H. Perry

There is a scene in the movie *The Poseidon Adventure* where the survivors are moving up a hallway toward the rear of a sinking ship when they meet another group heading down into the belly of the ship. The survivors try to get the group moving downward to turn around but are refused, and the downward group tells the group moving upward that they are wrong. Many times in life, a crowd is heading the wrong way but believes they are right and can't be convinced otherwise.

If you know you are right, then ignore the crowd! Like the old tale of lemmings to the sea, people will follow the leader to their death or to a disaster, blind to reality. This is what happens in cults or in groups like political parties. Use your head and intellect to recognize truth and reality. Blaze a trail to the real future instead of someone else's falsehood!

Day 102

"Put your foot upon the neck of the fear of criticism by reaching a decision not to worry about what other people think, do, or say."

—Napoleon Hill

Usually, people who criticize or naysay are ones who either failed and don't want you to succeed and make them look bad, or they are afraid to try and don't want you to succeed. Seldom will people encourage you to succeed when they haven't.

Too many people will also tell you that something can't be done. Science is often saying that things can't be done, and then someone comes along and proves that it *can* be done. People who live in a negative sphere don't think most things are possible simply because *they* can't do it. Most of my life, I have been told I could not do something, and that has made doing it a personal challenge. Then, when I did it, the person that said I couldn't usually just went away!

I remember one time, in the 1980s, I was looking for a color copier, and the head salesman at a local copy company told me that there was no such thing and that it was not possible for there ever to be such a thing. He said he had been in the business since copiers were invented and that he knew what he was talking about. A few years later, virtually every home in America had a color copier in it! I wanted to find the salesman and ask what had happened, but he had retired.

Don't listen to experts; they have a limited outlook!

Day 103

"Remember that the moment you reduce the statement of your desire and a plan for its realization to writing, you have actually taken the first of a series of steps, which will enable you to convert the thought into its physical counterpart."

—Napoleon Hill

Putting your dream in writing, on paper, is the first step to making it a reality. Somehow, when you actually write it out along with a plan to achieve it, you are transitioning it from a thought into a real thing. Now, you have a roadmap to follow.

The roadmap might change as you proceed, but you have something tangible in your hands. You have actually committed your dream to paper. You can take the roadmap out and look at it, redo parts of it, see it as reality, and start working toward the next step.

Get a piece of paper now. Write down your dream, describe it, and write a tentative plan to achieve it. Take the first step *NOW*!

Day 104

"Things may come to those who wait, but only the things left by those who hustle."

—Abraham Lincoln

You can wait, but you will be left behind by those who take action, and all you will have is the leftovers from the ones who acted. In case this wasn't clear to you before, the time to act is *NOW*! And the place to start is wherever you are! You already have the dream. The rest will fall into place as you move along.

All along in this book, I have promoted taking action, doing it now, and doing it wherever you are. There is a reason for that. It is because you have to get up and move out of your comfort zone. We are creatures of habit, and if we don't shake ourselves loose from our comfort zone, we will not move.

Don't let your dreams drift away because you won't move!

Part II: Days 101–200

Day 105

"Tact is the ability to describe others as they see themselves."

—Abraham Lincoln

When dealing with other people, you need to learn tact. Another description of tact that I once heard is that tact is the ability to tell a person to go to Hell and make them look forward to the trip.

Social skills in communication are essential to handling people you will deal with on the way to achieving your dreams. I am not promoting flattery or lying. But you need to learn to read people and converse with them in a way that will get them to best respond to you.

In the days before World War II, Dwight Eisenhower was an aide to General McArthur in the Philippines. McArthur was a great talker, and Eisenhower learned to listen attentively and give feedback to what McArthur said. McArthur commented that Eisenhower was a great conversationalist, but the truth was that Eisenhower was really a great listener. And sometimes, listening is the better part of a conversation!

Learn what is best when dealing with an individual based on the individual!

Day 106

"Big results require big ambitions."

—James Champy

Christopher Columbus had big ambitions. He wanted ships, provisions, and crews to sail to a new world. He wasn't interested in going where everyone else had been, and he found a new place to go.

John F. Kennedy set a goal of putting a man on the moon by the end of the 1960s when we barely had a capsule orbiting the planet. Big ambition, but it garnered big results. Sometimes, committing oneself to a big project motivates them to accomplish something they didn't think they could.

I once got involved in a sales business on the side, and one of the other people getting into it at the time went out and bought a new car. I asked him why, and he said it was his motivation to be successful. And he *was* successful!

Big ambitions will produce big results! What are *your* ambitions?

Part II: Days 101–200

Day 107

"The struggles we endure today will be the 'good old days' we laugh about tomorrow."

—Aaron Lauritsen

If we stick to our goals, that is! When I left home to join the Army, I had no idea what I would look back on in the years to come. I just knew I had ambitions and dreams. Now, I look back, and I have decades of great memories and happy memories from the Army, and they are the "good old days." But even today, I am still living some great days. I feel the best is yet to come because I haven't stopped thinking positively and looking forward to tomorrow!

I have gone through a divorce, but I met a better woman for me, whom I am still married to and happier than I ever dreamed possible. I went through a financial setback, but I recovered, and I am better off than I ever dreamed I would be and am getting better every day. I have post-traumatic stress disorder (PTSD), but thanks to my wife and the Lord above, I am living a happy life. I have a family I love, and I am able to help others. Life is good.

These days are the good old days!

Day 108

"All achievements, all earned riches, have their beginning in an idea."

—Andrew Carnegie

You cannot name one thing that does not fit this saying. Everything started as an idea! From an idea, it progressed into an action, and then it began taking shape either as a continued action (like an exploration) or as a physical item (like a machine). Then, it was maybe even marketed and created wealth through use by people.

Even money was a creation to be used to barter for goods and services. The value of some commodity like gold was established as an idea. But gold has no value unless we give it value.

A few centuries ago, tulip bulbs were traded and reached a value greater than gold. Like stocks in the stock market, they were valued, and then suddenly, the bulbs lost value and created a crash that destroyed fortunes. The stock market is an example of something that is of value only in your mind. The paper that is a stock is virtually worthless unless someone will buy it!

Ideas are what create value, achievements, and riches. Your dreams *can* become real and can create great riches!

Day 109

"What you're supposed to do when you don't like a thing is change it. If you can't change it, change the way you think about it. Don't complain."

—Maya Angelou

Well said! The easiest way to change something is to change the way you think about it. There are many variations on this, but the simplest is just to change how you feel about it.

If my house color offends you, don't fret over it; just learn to like it. See it from my perspective. Accept it as a unique variation in the neighborhood. Or maybe just quit thinking about it! We spend too much time worrying about other people's lives anyway. Live your own life, and concern yourself with *your* lifestyle. If you have a dream, focus on achieving it and not on my house paint.

Maya Angelo was a great woman of wisdom when it came to living together. Read her books. She wrote eloquent poems and stories. I never met her, but I wish I had.

Day 110

"Don't judge each day by the harvest you reap but by the seeds that you plant."

—Robert Louis Stevenson

So very true! It's what you put into life, not what you get out of it!

There are people—especially young people—who need examples to follow, words of wisdom, and mentoring. Set an example for others. Plant seeds of kindness and caring in what you do and say.

One practice I have is to strive to compliment people when they do good work. I don't care who they are or what they do; if they do a good job, appreciate them with a legitimate comment. Another good practice is that, if they have a name tag or nameplate, address them by name. And if you are unsure how to pronounce their name, ask them how. People appreciate that little effort, and it doesn't take much.

Another good practice is to tip people in service jobs where tipping is expected, even if the service is lousy. You don't know what is going on with them. The last customer might have been a total jerk, or their home life might be a disaster, or their boss might be on their butt. The tip might be what they need to jerk them back to reality!

Smile at people for no reason and say hello or good day. It might be the only nice thing they experience all day. Plant some seeds. It will make *you* feel better, too!

Part II: Days 101–200

Day 111

"It's kind of fun to do the impossible."

—Walt Disney

When my oldest grandson was about ten, his fondest wish was to get a real computer. But he knew that with his family's financial situation, that was not possible. My wife and I got hold of a computer and several side component games and wrapped them up for Christmas so that, when he would open the box, he would open the components first.

On Christmas morning, as my grandson was opening his presents, he opened some ordinary gifts, then one of the side components. He then opened another regular gift, then a control handle. He then opened another regular gift, then another component, and then he stopped, and his face changed. I still wish I had a video of that moment when he realized what he was opening and the look on his face went from surprise to "this can't be happening" to "it's a miracle." He started tearing the packages open, and his eyes were wide as saucers.

My wife and I felt like Walt Disney that day, thinking, *It's nice to do the impossible!* We've never had such a magical moment at any time since. I hope your dreams are like that for you!

Day 112

"Do not fear failure but rather fear not trying."

—Roy T. Bennett

Fear of failure is a reason many people choose not to try to achieve their dreams. But believe it or not, fear of succeeding is almost as great a fear. The responsibility of success is a hindrance to achieving a goal.

You should seriously consider the words of today's quote. In the long term of life, what will you live in regret of the most: having tried and failed or having never tried at all?

I have heard so many people in their later years lament about what they never did. I am so glad I don't have anything to cry about that I wanted to do and never tried to do. I changed some ambitions along the way in my life because something else came along, and I do sometimes wonder, *What if?* But I made a choice, and I have no regrets.

Take a shot at your dreams and desires. Travel to exotic places, climb a mountain, explore some remote place. Don't put off those desires because time passes faster than you realize when you get into living, and one day, you wake up, and it's too late!

Part II: Days 101–200

Day 113

"When the going gets tough, put one foot in front of the other and just keep going. Don't give up."

—Roy T. Bennett

When I was in the Special Forces (Green Berets), a friend of mine and I used to discuss the meaning of words. One such discussion was the difference between the words "endurance" and "stamina." We arrived at our own personal definitions, which were this:

- "Endurance" is the physical ability of your body to do something.
- "Stamina" is the mental ability to keep going once you've reached the limit of your endurance.

It might sound crazy, but sometimes, you reach your limit and can reach deep down inside yourself and make yourself just keep on going. That's the way it is when pursuing your dream! You might reach a point where you just can't go on anymore, but you will reach deep inside yourself and find that extra spark—that special desire that motivates you to go that extra step, then one more, then one more, until you reach your goal.

You don't know what I mean now. But when you get to that point, you will understand, and you will find that extra something deep down inside!

Day 114

"Start a huge, foolish project, like Noah. It makes absolutely no difference what people think of you."

—Rumi

They scoffed at Noah because nobody yet understood what rain was or what a flood was. But when the rain came, they all beat on the ark's doors to get in! People laughed at the Wright brothers, too. So, follow your dream, create something no one understands before you create it, and let them laugh.

I remember a man I knew whose daughter played softball with mine. He was in the banking business, and he moved into a new firm that handled credit cards. All his friends in conventional banking told him he was making a mistake and he should come back to the banking company. A few years later, his new company took off and became one of the most successful in the nation, and he was in the top three of the company. Suddenly, his former colleagues all wished they were in his shoes.

See the future, see what others don't, and create the future!

Part II: Days 101–200

Day 115

"Focus on your goals, not your fear. Focus like a laser beam on your goals."

—Roy T. Bennett

One thing I learned in golf—it took time and I still waiver sometimes—is to not look at the obstacles off the tee. Instead, I need to focus on the target area I want to hit my ball to. If I don't focus, and I let my mind wander to the water or sand or trees, that is where I will probably hit the ball. But if I focus just on the fairway landing area, I will probably hit the ball to the fairway landing area.

Focus on your dream and your goals like a laser. Don't let other people and other things distract you; they are not important. There will be enough issues along the way with your dream, so don't bring in outside issues to corrupt your dream.

Focus, set your sights, and go forward!

Day 116

"Adapt what is useful, reject what is useless, and add what is specifically your own."

—Bruce Lee

You can often get wisdom even from the most unexpected source. I was working with a young man one day, and he said he had a problem with a lot of preachers because they didn't always preach what he believed. I asked him how he dealt with that, and he said it was the same way he ate a steak: "I chew up the steak, swallow the meat, and spit out the bone."

Think about it. Just like today's quote says, all advice has something worthwhile. Even if the advice is something you don't want, you can probably mix it in with your own experiences and use it. I never forgot that young man's words.

Everything in life has the potential to be useful at some time or in some way. Use what you can, toss what's not useful, and blend what remains with your own ideas. That has been the pattern of man's creations since the beginning.

Day 117

"Luck is what happens when preparation meets opportunity."

—Seneca

Pro golfer Gary Player said that the more he practiced, the luckier he got. It holds true. The more you practice or prepare in any field, the luckier you get.

That is why I encourage you to do what it takes to prepare yourself to pursue your dream. If it means taking classes or going to the gym or participating in sports or whatever applies to your dream, do it! Apprentice in a field, do research . . . whatever. Do it so that you have the basic skills and knowledge to pursue the dream.

If you want to develop a holographic projector but have no understanding of holographics, you will have a hard time accomplishing your dream. Take classes, study the concepts, find out where science is at the time, and start from there.

Prepare yourself and go for it. You can start while you prepare, but . . . *prepare*!

Day 118

"Be steady and well-ordered in your life so that you can be fierce and original in your work."

—Gustave Flaubert

Plan and organize your life so that things are well-ordered and fairly predictable. Eliminate surprises on a daily basis so that you can be dedicated to your dream and a passionate pursuit of it.

Like a runner trying to set a new record, you don't want debris all over the track tripping you up as you try to run faster and faster. You don't want daily activities muddling your life up as you pursue your dream. You need to be able to focus on the dream and the work necessary to accomplish it rather than on day-to-day matters.

Keep your life simple, and keep your mind fiercely focused on your goal!

Part II: Days 101–200

Day 119

"Don't say you don't have enough time. You have exactly the same number of hours per day that were given to Helen Keller, Pasteur, Michelangelo, Mother Teresa, Leonardo da Vinci, Thomas Jefferson, and Albert Einstein."

—H. Jackson Brown Jr.

Decades ago, I stopped saying I didn't have time, and I started being honest with myself by saying, "I didn't *take* time." That is the truth in almost every case! We don't program our time and use it wisely, and so we don't get things done that we should or could.

We have time to watch a four-hour football game but not enough time to do a fifteen-minute report. We can talk mindlessly on the phone for hours or play video games but can't work for an hour on a project or write a paper or book. The fact is, we make time for what we want to do, even if it is a waste of time!

One reason I advocate making a list each day of what you want to accomplish is that it focuses your attention and allocates your time. You tend to get more done in less time and begin organizing your day overall. If you put your dream into a plan and your plan into a goal with time phases, you begin scheduling your time and getting more done!

Day 120

"Don't be pushed around by the fears in your mind. Be led by the dreams in your heart."

—Roy T. Bennett

Your mind will try to create fears and doubts based on what other people have said and will say. What you have been taught and read and what the "experts" have declared will create serious doubts! But you have to realize that your dream is unique and is there to create a new path, a new way, a new idea. So, those *old* tried and true ways and ideas are not the final answer.

Listen to your heart; your dream is there for a reason. Even if you fail a thousand times, use those failures to learn what doesn't work and try a new way, a new approach. You might be just a tiny little way off from perfecting your dream. Just try one more time— just . . . one . . . more . . . time!

It worked for Edison. It worked for Marconi. It worked for Ford. It *will* work for you!

Part II: Days 101–200

Day 121

"Do what you can, with what you have, where you are."

—Theodore Roosevelt

When David faced Goliath, he didn't wait until someone invented a rifle. Instead, he took his sling, picked up five smooth stones, and faced Goliath in the riverbed.

David knew he had God on his side, and he knew he had practiced with his sling for years. He had used it against bears and other critters, and he could hit a target with great accuracy. He had self-confidence, and he didn't listen to other people, and he sure didn't listen to the big-mouthed Goliath!

David didn't stand around second-guessing his decision. Instead, he took off running at Goliath, whirling his sling with a stone in it, and he whipped it straight at Goliath's forehead. Now, if you've read the story, he didn't kill Goliath with the sling, but he did knock that big ugly out. And then he pulled Goliath's own sword and chopped Goliath's head off. *That* finished Goliath off!

Do what you can, with what you have, where you are. You *will* succeed!

Day 122

"And when you want something, the entire universe conspires in helping you to achieve it."

—Paulo Coelho

It seems that when the true achiever decides they want something and sets about to get it, the whole world falls in step to help them achieve their goals. Once you find your dream, find your goal, establish your plan, and set about to pursue that dream, it seems the whole world begins to fall in place to help you achieve your purpose. People begin to appear with the knowledge and skills that can help you develop your goals. Others have assets that will support your endeavors. And still others provide locations you can work in.

One by one, your needs are met. When needed, someone comes along to assist you. The universe provides for your needs as you fulfill your destiny!

Part II: Days 101–200

Day 123

"What lies behind us and what lies before us are tiny matters compared to what lies within us."

—Ralph Waldo Emerson

Your past is gone, and whatever you did, good or bad, doesn't matter. The future is yet to come, and no one knows what will be. The one thing you can control is what you have inside of you! All of us actually have the same opportunities in life, regardless of who we were born to or where we were born. It's just a matter of what we are willing to try!

Dr. Ben Carson is one of the leading surgeons in America and has served on the staff of a US president. BUT! He was born and raised by a single-parent mother in a poor project. By all social norms, he should be a failure—a criminal, a drug addict, and on welfare. That's what society probably labeled him for. But his mother had other ideas and taught him that he had opportunities. He took those opportunities and became successful and *highly* respected! He wasn't born special, and what he did to become special should be the norm for everyone.

I was also raised poor by a single-parent mother in the projects, and I quit high school my senior year. I joined the Army, finished my education, got a college degree (graduating *magna cum laude*), became an officer, served in elite Army units to include the Old Guard (which put me in the White House, around the President and other high-level people), and I saw the world. I have accomplished things my fellow high school classmates never dreamed of because I saw opportunity, and I took it.

Look inside yourself and grasp whatever opportunities you can!

Day 124

> "Attitude is a choice. Happiness is a choice. Optimism is a choice. Kindness is a choice. Giving is a choice. Respect is a choice. Whatever choice you make makes you. Choose wisely."
>
> —Roy T. Bennett

The CEO of that corporation is there because of choices they made. That homeless person on the street is often—though not always—there because of choices they made. The convict in prison is there because of choices they made. The worker living a regular life is there because of choices they made.

You are the end result of all the choices you have made, and your future will be the result of the choices you make from here on out. So, make those choices wisely! Not happy with where you are? Then choose to make a change—a better job, or self-employment, or take classes to change professions. Make a choice!

You are never too old to make a choice that can change your life. Grandma Moses started painting in her 80s! Who says you have to retire at sixty-five . . . or *ever*? Maybe you went to college to be a computer programmer but will be happier as a plumber. It's *your* choice!

Part II: Days 101–200

Day 125

"Most obstacles melt away when we make up our minds to walk boldly through them."

—Orison Swett Marden

Oh my, how true! One acronym for the word fear is:

- F: False
- E: Evidence
- A: Appearing
- R: Real

Sometimes, what seems to be an insurmountable obstacle is really a mirage that was created in your own mind by what other people tell you or by you blowing something out of proportion. When I met my wife, she had been struggling for years, taking classes to get her high school diploma (when she was younger, she had been forced to quit school and care for her brothers). She was tackling the diploma like it was a mountain. I convinced her to just go take the GED, telling her that if she failed it, it wouldn't stop her, but if she passed it, then she could go on and take college classes.

She took the GED and passed with good scores. (She's really a smart lady!) Soon, she was pursuing a degree in computer programming. And that obstacle just disappeared when she walked straight through it! Once she conquered that, she was unstoppable.

Just do it!

Day 126

"It is not the mountain we conquer but ourselves."

—Edmund Hillary

I told you earlier about me and jump school. What I didn't tell you is that I was a bit afraid of heights, and when I was facing my first jump training at the thirty-four-foot tower, I hesitated, staring down at the ground in fear. The tower's non-commissioned officer booted me off the tower, and after that, jumping became fun. I had—with a little help from the boot—conquered the fear inside of me. The tower didn't change; I did. After that, jumping wasn't a problem, and that carried over to rappelling and to all the other great things I got to do. I learned that it's what's inside of me that has to be overcome that matters to success.

One of the greatest fears people face is public speaking. So, when I was first tasked with teaching a class, I had that gut-twisting feeling of having to stand in front of dozens of people and talk. I went into a latrine (which is Army for bathroom), and I stood in front of a mirror and taught myself the class. Try it for yourself. When you can speak to yourself with a straight face, speaking to other people is a cinch. After my first class, I was at ease teaching.

Learn to conquer *yourself*, and the rest is easy!

Day 127

"Do what you feel in your heart to be right—for you'll be criticized anyway."

—Eleanor Roosevelt

There's an old expression, "Damned if you do, damned if you don't." So true! No matter what path you choose, there are those who will criticize your choices. So, do what is right in your heart.

They criticized Jesus, and they will criticize you. All innovators are criticized, even when they are right. So, follow your dream and ignore the naysayers! The naysayers still think Earth is flat and the sun revolves around Earth.

Day 128

"You never fail until you stop trying."

—Albert Einstein

Legendary football coach Vince Lombardi famously said, "A winner never quits, and a quitter never wins!" Truer words have never been spoken. Every great breakthrough is from someone who refuses to give up. No one ever said success is easy. If it were, everyone would be a great success. The reason the history books are limited to a few chosen names is that most people quit early, and only a few kept at it until they succeeded.

Did you ever wonder why there are small settlements in the middle of nowhere? Sometimes, it's because settlers gave up and settled where they were instead of continuing to move on until they reached the best place. Don't quit. Take a break if you must but get back at it and finish the pursuit of your dream. The end result is worth it!

Part II: Days 101–200

Day 129

"The wisest mind has something yet to learn."

—George Santayana

I have a fond memory of my oldest grandson on the day he graduated from kindergarten. He proudly posed with his diploma and declared, "I are a graduate; I don't have to go to school anymore!" Boy, was he surprised!

No one ever reaches the point that they don't have something new to learn, that an experience won't enlighten them, or that an outlook on something won't reveal new possibilities. The greatest minds know they don't know it all. When I meet someone who thinks they know everything and are so educated that they look down on others, I know I have met a foolish person—someone who will soon stumble from their own ignorance. You must stay open to new ideas and new knowledge. The world is moving ahead so fast that your education is outdated before you graduate!

One old commercial for a computer used to express it best. The consumer was shown smugly driving home with the latest model computer when he looks up at a billboard that announces the introduction of the next, new, upgraded model of that computer. That's how life is: just as we grasp number one, number two is here!

Remain open to learning, or you will become outdated!

Day 130

"You can if you think you can."

—George Reeves

Remember the children's story about the little engine that could? It had to climb a steep hill, and, try as it might, it couldn't. But it had to in order to rescue the people. So, as it struggled, it repeated over and over, "I think I can, I think I can, I think I can . . ." And it did!

And that's how *you* have to be! Don't doubt, believe. *I think I can.* Or even better: *I KNOW I can!*

At the homeless ministry I worked with some years ago, they held interviews to decide which homeless people to let into the program. One man had no way to get to the interview, so he went to a blood bank and gave blood for money. Then, he bought a six-pack of soda with the money and sold the sodas by the can and used that money for bus fare to get to the interview so that he could get into the program. I called him the "I can man." There is always a way if you think you can!

Day 131

"Don't wait. The time will never be just right."

—Napoleon Hill

If you wait for the time to be right, you will die waiting! You will always have an excuse why it's not the right time.

The time is *NOW*! No matter what is missing, start anyway—the missing pieces will come along. Need money? Start with what you have, and the money will appear eventually. Need help? Start now, and the help will come. Need space? Start now, and eventually, you will find more space.

Just start, and whatever you are missing will eventually appear!

Day 132

"Tough times never last, but tough people do."

—Dr. Robert Schuller

I've seen many people break during tough times and lose out on the rewards they were striving for. Many people I thought going in would hang tough because of their backgrounds and experience surprisingly fell away fast.

When I went through Office Candidate School, there were many prior service people like myself—men who had combat experience and were non-commissioned officers with years of experience. I assumed they would do well and tough it out with ease. But to my surprise, most of them dropped out by the end of the eighth week! They could not adjust to being harassed and bossed around by the tactical officers. The new guys, with less experience, fared much better and earned my respect for toughing it out.

As the old saying goes: when the going gets tough, the tough get going!

Part II: Days 101–200

Day 133

"My mission in life is not merely to survive but to thrive."

—Maya Angelou

There's a line in the first *Rambo* movie (called *First Blood*) that really describes the tough and survivor types. When Rambo's former commander is talking to the sheriff, he describes Rambo's personality by saying, "What you call Hell, he calls home."

Survivors will thrive in tough environments. Survivors adapt and grow, capitalizing on the stress and hardship, seeing gain where others see loss. In the great depression, when many were losing everything and going under, the survivors saw opportunity and made great fortunes. Survivors don't just survive; they *thrive* under pressure!

The greats in history—the men who built America—thrived under pressure and created vast dynasties under the worst conditions. Be a thriver!

Day 134

"You must do the things you think you cannot do."

—Eleanor Roosevelt

The Army, and specifically the Special Forces, taught me what I could really do. It pushed me to my limits and then pushed me to surpass my limits. If my best was to run five miles, then they ran me ten. I carried seventy or eighty pounds or more on my back and walked cross-country through swamps until I thought I was going to drop and then more. And when we got to our objective, we attacked a target.

In the Army, we were pushed not only to our physical limits but also to our mental limits and usually to both at the same time. And we were then, at that point, expected to function at peak performance. It was invigorating to find out what I could really do!

You will be amazed at the things you can do that you think you cannot do!

Day 135

"There is only one way to happiness, and that is to cease worrying about things which are beyond our power or our will."

—Epictetus

There are things you can control and things you cannot control. Learn which is which! Leave those things that are beyond your control to those who can control them or to God and focus on what you *can* control. Your life will be so much simpler!

Worry is wasted mental energy and time. If something is out of your control, worry won't change it. So, just accept it, and do what you can. Odds are it will not be an issue. And if it does become an issue, then take action.

"What if" is a negative idea that can derail the best plans you can make. There is a flip side to "what if something bad happens," which is "what if something bad *doesn't* happen?" So, quit worrying over things that you can't control and probably won't happen anyway!

Day 136

"As I grow older, I pay less attention to what men say. I just watch what they do."

—Andrew Carnegie

Talk is cheap; *action* is what matters! Politicians are always saying what they will do if elected, and then, when they become elected, they seem to suffer from amnesia. Most people make promises then renege on their promises because it's too hard to follow through.

If you want to be known as a person of character, do what you say you are going to do. First off, it will totally surprise everyone. Second, it will give you a reputation as being a person of your word. And that is a rare commodity in our times!

If you live a life in which people *see* what you are, then you don't have to talk about yourself!

Day 137

"Success can be attained in any branch of labor. There's always room at the top in every pursuit."

—Andrew Carnegie

Long ago, I was talking with my grandson about being a success, and he was concerned that he couldn't be a CEO or someone of such stature. I told him that being in such a high-up position is not the only measure of success and that being the best at what you choose to be is the real measure of success. I told him that if he chose to be a garbage collector, and he was the best garbage collector in town, then he was a success. If he chose to be a computer programmer, and he was the best at that, then he was a success.

My grandson being the best at whatever he chose to do would make him a success. And me telling him that seemed to take the pressure of succeeding off him. I meant what I told him. Being the best at what you choose is the real measure of success.

If you become the CEO, and you aren't very good at it, then you *aren't* a success—you are either lucky or related to the owner!

Day 138

"It marks a big step in your development when you come to realize that other people can help you do a better job than you could do alone."

—Andrew Carnegie

Read, as I have suggested many times so far, Napoleon Hill's book *Think and Grow Rich*. He learned most of what he wrote from associating with Andrew Carnegie. And he refers to the gathering of many people together to create a "brain trust" as the "mastermind."

General Eisenhower often said that he was not a great leader, but he knew how to surround himself with great men who could advise him. His staff during World War II was made up of some of the greatest military minds of the time.

No great leader or corporate manager does it all alone. They all pick a staff of experts to advise and assist in creating whatever they are doing. Learn from their practice and learn to identify people you can work with to reach your dream most efficiently!

Part II: Days 101–200

Day 139

"Ambition is a dream with a V8 engine. Ain't nowhere else in the world where you can go from driving a truck to a Cadillac overnight."

—Elvis Presley

Ambition combined with hard work will take you from zero to sixty in a flash! In every field, you see people going from unknowns to superstars in rapid order. Entertainers, sports figures, and business entrepreneurs alike are all rising so fast it is scary.

People like Jeff Bezos built an empire from a small startup in a garage to a mega billion-dollar business in less than half a lifetime. And some technology social media billionaires have done it by their twenties and early thirties. It is mind-boggling. But it's all possible for anyone who has a dream and pursues it with a fiery passion!

Day 140

"Am I not destroying my enemies when I make friends of them?"

—Abraham Lincoln

Now *that* is a unique idea! How better to eliminate your enemies than to make them your friends? Take those trying to stop you and those creating roadblocks and get them on your side. Now, they are clearing a path for you and accelerating your progress. Instead of criticizing you, they are applauding. And instead of holding you back, they are supporting. What a great scheme—turn your enemy into your friend. That will teach them!

Part II: Days 101–200

Day 141

"Always bear in mind that your own resolution to succeed is more important than any other."

—Abraham Lincoln

It doesn't matter what others think, yay or nay! Your mother can think you are the greatest and that your idea is better than sliced bread, but if you do not have the same or better resolution and dedication than others, then it is all for naught.

Edison's mother didn't perfect the light bulb. Galileo's father didn't develop his ideas on gravity. Ford's wife didn't refine the assembly line. Harlan Sanders's cousin didn't fry the chicken. They all had the driving desire and dedication to follow their dream and complete their destinies. Do *you*?

Day 142

"Cherish your vision and your dreams as they are the children of your soul, the blueprints of your ultimate achievements."

—Napoleon Hill

Your dreams and visions are your personal creations—your innermost personal ideas. No one else in all of creation will ever have the exact same ideas and potential as you. And if you do not follow through, you might be depriving all of humanity of some great creation for all time!

Imagine history without the invention of the airplane. Or what if the telephone had never been created? How would we build great bridges and skyscrapers if Bessemer had not created a way to refine iron into steel?! What would the history of man have been without the pet rock???

Well, maybe that last one we could have lived without. But you get my drift. Your dream might be the next great leap in technology and humankind's great breakthrough!

Day 143

"Dreams are the seedlings of reality."

—Napoleon Hill

Everything we have today or that has existed throughout time started out as an idea—a dream in someone's mind. Someone saw a need for something or possibly envisioned the "something" itself and then set about making it a reality.

It is hard to believe, but that smartphone you use daily was once just an idea in Steve Jobs's mind. And the computer you use daily was once just an idea in someone's mind. Your car was once an inconceivable item, but someone conceived it as an idea, and today, we drive them routinely.

If you can dream it, it will someday be a reality!

Day 144

"Every adversity, every failure, every heartbreak, carries with it the seed of an equal or greater benefit."

—Napoleon Hill

You will hopefully soon realize that every adversity is actually a step on the staircase to success. Every trial, every failure, every heartbreak is actually a lesson on a map to a breakthrough. You almost look forward to the next failure or obstacle because it will lead you to your next leap ahead!

You don't really want failures, but you learn that they are not terminal and that they can be beneficial. You see their benefits, and you begin to learn from them quickly and turn them around to your advantage. Soon, your progress is like a stock market chart—a series of up and down spikes, with the center line showing the steady upward progression.

You are making progress!

Part II: Days 101–200

Day 145

"My great concern is not whether you have failed but whether you are content with your failure."

—Abraham Lincoln

Herein lays the crux of the matter: have you languished in your failure? Are you satisfied in having at least tried but failed?

Failure is a step on the path, but it is not the destination! Never be content with failure. Instead, learn from it and move ahead with another effort. Keep moving on, learning as you go until you reach the pinnacle of success!

Alexander Graham Bell didn't quit when he failed to get an answer on his last experiment. He kept trying until he got a response. And today, we have telephones. Edison didn't quit when the last filament would not last more than a few minutes. He kept at it. And today, we have functioning light bulbs.

You must keep at it until your dream is a real, functioning, and viable reality!

Day 146

"Ambition is the path to success. Persistence is the vehicle you arrive in."

—Bill Bradley

Persistence is the key to achieving every goal in life! Want to be a great golfer? You must practice, practice, practice and play, play, play. Persistence is the key!

The same holds true if you want to be a great singer, or a great actor, or a great orator, or a great manager. No matter what you want to be good at, you must be persistent! If you are following a dream and working on a goal, an invention, or a great idea, persistence is the key. Your dream becomes your driving force, your obsession, and your life's purpose. You live to complete the dream.

Study the great people of history, and the one thing that sticks out above all else as a common denominator is . . . *persistence*!

Day 147

"I wish to have as my epitaph: Here lies a man who was wise enough to bring into his service men who knew more than he."

—Andrew Carnegie

This was one of Carnegie's greatest strengths and contributed to his great success. He sought those who knew the most in their field and would work together to achieve a common goal. He nurtured the "mastermind" concept and focused the people around him toward his common dream. So, it is no wonder that Carnegie built a giant, successful empire in the steel industry and became the richest man in the world in his time.

Strength in unity and greatness in unifying the knowledge and skills of many—use it to your advantage!

Day 148

"It is impossible for a man to learn what he thinks he already knows."

—Epictetus

The saddest thing is a mind closed to new learning. Throughout time, so many great people have reached the point where they thought they knew it all, and at that point, they began their decline. You will never be so educated or informed on any subject that you cannot learn something new.

Only fools think they know it all. No matter how well educated you are in any given subject, there is always something new to learn about it!

Day 149

> "He is a wise man who does not grieve for the things which he has not but rejoices for those which he has."
>
> —Epictetus

Appreciate and rejoice in what you have. There are those who would give all they have to have what you do. There are always those with less. So, learn not only to appreciate what you have but also to function and advance with what you have. Sometimes, having little motivates you to strive harder, to improvise, and to be more creative. You can develop greater ideas and methods when you are not handicapped by having all the easy ways at your disposal.

Take what you have and run with it!

Day 150

"We are not disturbed by what happens to us but by our thoughts about what happens to us."

—Epictetus

How we perceive what happens is more important than what actually happens. In any given situation, watch how different people react to what occurs around them.

When my grandson was a small toddler, we had a system of reacting to his incidents that lessened his stress. When he would fall or bump himself, we would try to act as if nothing had happened or as if it was simply ok. He would watch our faces and reactions and would usually react according to our reaction. Even when he was hurt, he often would not cry or act hurt if we just acted like it was nothing. But when his mother was around, she would usually overreact, and he would panic and scream and cry at even the minor bumps.

It's how we react to a situation that usually dictates the circumstances and not the situation itself!

Day 151

"Impossible is for the unwilling."

—John Keats

When I was in Vietnam during the war, we had a sign in our base camp that said: *The impossible we do right away. Miracles just take a little longer.* If you are willing to do what other people are not, then you can do almost anything!

My favorite scripture is one that goes: *All things are possible to those who believe.* If you believe, especially in yourself, things can be accomplished. The problem for most people is that they don't believe in themselves. People lack self-confidence and the willingness to work or to try something that might be difficult or take them out of their comfort zone.

Don't be like the crowd. Be unique and do the impossible!

Day 152

"Dream big and dare to fail."

—Norman Vaughan

Anyone can dream small dreams and take little chances. But only great people dream big dreams and take big chances. Failure is often the result of big chances, but big risks bring big rewards, and big lessons are learned from big failures.

The Wright brothers could have stayed on the ground with their bicycles, but they had big dreams, and they took big chances. If they had failed, it could have cost them their lives. But they went for it anyway! Our greatest explorers were not sure they would return alive, but they went ahead anyway, too.

Be bold, dream big, and venture forth boldly!

Part II: Days 101–200

Day 153

"Life is like riding a bicycle. To keep your balance, you must keep moving."

—Albert Einstein

All throughout history, people have settled for less than the best because they quit where they were and stopped moving! Settlers grew tired of traveling and stopped to establish towns in the middle of nowhere instead of going on and finding the ideal lands. Businesses quit growing because the owners grew tired of the work or the risk and settled for being a small shop instead of a big business. People stopped trying and settled for being just a cog in the big wheel instead of moving up and running the operation or building their own business.

Don't stop and settle for less. Keep moving and establish your place in life. Grab hold of life and build the best you can!

Day 154

"All our dreams come true if we have the courage to pursue them."

—Walt Disney

There are so many people who have great dreams but allow other people to stifle those dreams by filling them with all the reasons they can't achieve them! Somewhere out there are great writers who never wrote their novels. And there are great artists who never painted their portraits. And there are great doctors who never practiced medicine. There are so many great people who never were because someone destroyed their dreams with negative words! Someone crushed their courage and filled them with doubt.

The greatest thing we can do is find someone with a great dream and be their encourager. Lift them up and help them find the way. Build their courage and back them along their journey. Part of that will be by achieving success ourselves and then coming back for others!

Sometimes, all someone needs is a mentor who believes in them. Be there for someone!

Day 155

"The mind is its own place and in itself can make a heaven of hell, a hell of heaven."

—John Milton

In the book *Paradise Lost*, Milton documents the journey of a pilgrim through Hell. Satan is quoted as saying he would rather rule in Hell than serve in Heaven.

Many of us have that same attitude, and we lose out on the rewards that humility and correct attitudes can bring us in life. Our mental outlooks can change how we perceive our surroundings and how we live our lives. If we are in rebellion, Heaven can be Hell. But if we are at peace with our surroundings, we can make Hell a Heaven!

What is *your* attitude?

Day 156

"Overcome the notion that you must be regular. It robs you of the chance to be extraordinary."

—Uta Hagen

Too often, people think they have to conform to the crowd and just "fit in." When we do, we lose our uniqueness and begin to become just ordinary—a copy of everyone else. But we are not meant to be a cookie-cutter copy of the people around us. Instead, we were created different—fearfully and wonderfully made.

Each of us has unique chromosomes. We have DNA that is separate from anyone else in the world. Our fingerprints are not like anyone else's either. We are special, and our personalities are supposed to be also.

You are extraordinary and should practice being so. You have dreams and ideas that are special to you. You have talents and gifts that no one else has, and you have contributions to the world that we need!

Don't conform to the world. Give us your uniqueness so that we can benefit from you!

Day 157

"We can do anything we want to if we stick to it long enough."

—Helen Keller

Succeeding is oftentimes just a matter of sticking to it long enough! Dwight Eisenhower was a major for many, many years—long enough to be almost a full career to some people. But in the end, he jumped from major to four-star general in a flash. Hanging in there pays off, and the best rise to the top eventually! Eisenhower was a colonel and an aide to Major General Patton, but a few years later, he was a five-star general commanding Patton in World War II.

Never quit because you feel you have failed or are unappreciated! As an enlisted soldier, I was the senior private first class because I was carrying the radio for my platoon leader, and the platoon sergeant didn't value my job. But later, a new platoon sergeant recognized my talent, and a first sergeant sent me up for sergeant ahead of many senior people. With that, I zoomed past all the ones who had been promoted ahead of me.

Stick with it. Your day will come!

Day 158

"Get to the point where you get allergic to average! You don't think average!"

—Eric Thomas

Average is a dime a dozen and not worth that! Be what you are worth and do your best. And soon, you will get rewarded for *your* worth and not what others are worth.

In any occupation, the average worker wants you to be like them so that they don't look bad. They will try to convince you that trying doesn't pay off and that you are wasting your time being above average. Do not listen! Do your best each and every day. Study to get better and do not get discouraged. The bosses are watching, and when they see you are consistent, they will promote you ahead of the herd!

The average will be resentful. But always remember that they don't pay your bills, and they don't feed your family, and they sure don't have your dreams. Average is easy. Above-average is where you want to be!

Day 159

"If I cannot do great things, I can do small things in a great way."

—Martin Luther King Jr.

There's an old saying: How do you eat an elephant? One bite at a time!

Most great accomplishments are not done all at once. Instead, they are a series of small accomplishments done consistently. Do each task to the best of your ability and do them consistently. Build on each success and watch your greatness grow. Ford didn't open a massive business at once; he started out with a series of factories and grew his empire.

Grow your dream in a *series* of successes. Do each small task in a great way each day!

Day 160

"Be faithful to that which exists within yourself."

—André Gide

You are the origin and pursuer of your dreams. Be faithful to what is within yourself. Follow your dreams and ensure they are created because no one else will or can.

The book you are reading is a simple thing and is the collection and amplification of many other people's wisdom. But the compilation and amplification are *my* dream, not theirs. It came to me as the result of a need I felt, first for myself and then as a daily message to a small circle of friends and then as what I felt others could benefit from.

The world suffers from negativism and poor self-esteem, and I want to contribute to overcoming that. We are worth more than that. God gave us the power of love, a sound mind, and the ability to overcome fears. A positive outlook on life is how we overcome!

Become faithful to that which lies within you. You are a positive being with a power of positivity that can overcome negative thoughts!

Part II: Days 101–200

Day 161

"People are not disturbed by things but by the views they take of them."

—Epictetus

This quote is a variation on what has been said many times throughout this book: things do not affect you, but how you view those things disturbs you. If you wake up and it is raining, the rainy day doesn't disturb you; it is how you view that rainy day. It can be an, "Oh no, I'm going to get wet! Traffic is going to be bad!" Or you can see it as, "The yard needs rain. This will clear the atmosphere. I love the smell of rain."

If traffic is bad, you can see it as, "I'm going to be stuck in traffic!" Or instead, maybe as, "This is a great chance to listen to that motivational tape!" Or maybe you just got a "no" on that sale you thought you had. It can be, "Oh no, I lost another sale!" Or instead, as Zig Ziglar would say, "Oh boy, I am one step closer to another yes!"

Don't let things bother you. See a good side to them and rejoice!

Day 162

"There is little success where there is little laughter."

—Andrew Carnegie

This is a key to positive thinking and positive action: positive people laugh a lot. Humor is abundant when you see the positive side of life. Failure isn't devastating, and success is invigorating. You learn to laugh at yourself and *with* other people, not at other people!

The world is a happier place to live in and you are a happier person to be around when there is laughter!

Part II: Days 101–200

Day 163

"Don't be afraid to be ambitious about your goals. Hard work never stops. Neither should your dreams."

—Dwayne Johnson

People are willing to get up and go to work at oh-dark-thirty and work hard all day, come home, and get ready to do it again the next day for a minimal salary. And yet, they are unwilling to give an effort for their dreams. It's amazing that we give our all for someone else's fortunes and dreams but not our own!

Put some of your precious and limited time into your own dreams and goals. Work for yourself as hard as you do for others. You are worth it, and your dreams and goals are definitely worth it.

Instead of coming home and flopping down on the couch, spend some time working on your dreams. Put in some time on your future. If you do, one day, you will get up and go to work for yourself, and others will be working for you!

Live for your dreams!

Day 164

"Don't worry when you are not recognized but strive to be worthy of recognition."

—Abraham Lincoln

You might not always be recognized. Most people will be jealous of your success and will try to hide your successes. Regardless, you are not really seeking recognition. Instead, you are seeking to achieve your dreams and accomplish your goals. And if you are successful, others will see your success.

    You just need to do what you do with integrity and do it in a manner worthy of recognition. Sometimes greatness is recognized in history but not in the present. So, never resent the fact that others fail to recognize your accomplishments. You know what you have done, and if your accomplishments have benefitted others, that is what matters!

Part II: Days 101–200

Day 165

"Desire is the starting point of all achievement—not a hope, not a wish, but a keen pulsating desire which transcends everything."

—Napoleon Hill

It is imperative for you to realize that wishing is not the key and hoping is not the key but getting a heart-burning desire *is* the key! You need to make a decision that you are in—and that means *all* in. Your dream is worth it! It is your ticket to your future. And if you want to be the success you are meant to be, then you must commit to your dream with a passion.

The road is littered with halfhearted people who tried and quit. But you need to be a full-time, all-out success. The difference between a Michael Jordan and a might-have-been is that heart-burning desire!

Day 166

"An intangible impulse of thought can be transmuted into material rewards."

—Napoleon Hill

I've said it many times so far: everything we use—every invention, every idea—has started out as a thought in someone's mind. And then it became their obsession, and then a goal, and then a tangible idea or object!

This book started out that way. Your smartphone started out that way. Your TV started out that way. The chair you are sitting in did, the house you are in did, and the car you drive did. And so on and so on. And each one of those items resulted in material rewards for the person who created them!

Your dreams will manifest as a reality that will manifest rewards for you!

Day 167

"A quitter never wins, and a winner never quits."

—Vince Lombardi

Simple and straightforward! There are millions—perhaps billions—of quitters in history who you never heard of. Why? Because they *quit*! And there are a limited number of winners you know about. Why? Because they never quit!

We know about the Wright brothers, Alexander Graham Bell, and Thomas Edison because they did not quit. And even the less noble who never quit are famous. We know about people like Napoleon, Hitler, Genghis Khan, etc., not because they were great and noble but because they did not quit. There were millions—perhaps billions—of people in history who tried and quit, and no one knows them.

Be a winner. Do not quit!

Day 168

"There is no substitute for persistence. The person who makes persistence his watchword discovers that 'Old Man Failure' finally becomes tired and makes his departure. Failure cannot cope with persistence."

—Napoleon Hill

Keep it up! Never cease! Failure will grow weary and finally quit, becoming the loser, and you will be the winner.

Persist, persist, and persist! Write the word down and put it on your mirrors. Keep it in your wallet. Let it be the one word you repeat every day. Take the word "can't" out of your vocabulary and replace it with "persist." You can! You . . . *can*!

Persistence is all you need to succeed!

Day 169

"Both success and failure are largely the results of habit!"

—Napoleon Hill

Amen! What you do on a daily basis—your daily habits—will ultimately determine your success or failure. That means you have to develop habits that will lead you to a successful end result. Being on time, following up, completing tasks, being reliable, etc.

Don't procrastinate! Successful people are organized, and they utilize their time efficiently. You can study successful people and develop good habits. Find out what bad habits you have and break them, and then replace them with good ones. Psychologists say it takes just six weeks to break or make a habit.

Study yourself and track your habits!

Day 170

"If you are not learning while you're earning, you are cheating yourself out of the better portion of your compensation."

—Napoleon Hill

While you are working, and especially if you are in the field your dreams are related to, you should be learning everything you can about that field. Learn the technical and administrative aspects. Learn where they get the financing and logistical support. Study the marketing plans and distribution systems. Learn everything you can—it will give you a massive head start on your goals.

Even if you are not specifically in the field you will be working toward, the supporting areas will be similar and can save you immense effort down the road. In addition, you might identify people you can call on or utilize to help you in your endeavors later on. Carnegie grew up working for a man in the railroad industry, and Carnegie learned everything he could about business and about building with iron and steel. It helped him eventually create the greatest steel empire in the world!

Plan ahead and learn as you go!

Part II: Days 101–200

Day 171

"No man will make a great leader who wants to do it all himself or get all the credit for doing it."

—Andrew Carnegie

You might have to start alone. But realize that you will have to include others to gain outside expertise, manpower, and growth. Henry Ford needed thousands of workers of all types to create his empire. Carnegie used men from all walks of life to build his empire, and he gave credit to them for their contributions and shared the wealth with them as he grew.

Great corporations are not one-person operations, and they aren't the credit of one person. So, learn to build and utilize teams! Great leaders surround themselves with people who are experts in various fields related to the business that they are building.

Day 172

"People who are unable to motivate themselves must be content with mediocrity, no matter how impressive their other talents."

—Andrew Carnegie

You are the most important person you will ever motivate! If you aren't motivated about your dream or goal, then no one else around you will be motivated about it either. Who will care much for your dreams and goals if *you* seem to care little for them? You must be enthusiastic and excited about the potential, even when it seems there is nothing happening.

I once heard it best from a man at an advertising bureau when he said, "I sell the sizzle, not the steak." Sometimes, the idea is a little dull, but what the idea can do or how it can be attractive is what you need to sell, especially to your team. You must sell the sizzle!

Part II: Days 101–200

Day 173

> "Attach yourself to what is spiritually superior, regardless of what other people think or do. Hold to your true aspirations no matter what is going on around you."
>
> —Epictetus

Don't sell out to the world to get by! Your character and integrity are the only things you have that are not for sale, and in the process of pursuing your dream, you must keep them intact. People will try to short-circuit your reputation and buy out your dreams for their own gain, but . . . don't let them! Maintain your goals and go for your dream with character. Don't sell yourself out, and don't sell your dreams out.

The world needs what you have to offer, not some cheap version that some shyster wants to make a buck off. It might be hard, especially when your finances are tight. But you can do it. There is a reason the dream was given to *you*!

Day 174

"Leave no stone unturned."

—Euripides

Too often, people assume they have looked at every option, but they have missed the obvious. The reason is usually because they have limited themselves to what conventional thinking says will work. You must get out of the box and try something that convention says *won't* work as it just might be the answer!

The reason new and unique ideas are being discovered is because they are new and unique. As I mentioned earlier in this book, I once read that in the late 1800s, science said men couldn't travel over twenty-five miles an hour because they couldn't breathe at speeds faster than that. Wrong! They also said that if women traveled at thirty miles an hour and stopped too fast, their ovaries would fly out of their bodies. Wrong again! Science is great, but it has a reputation for erroneous ideas.

Think outside the box and ignore the experts. You will invent more new and unique things that way!

Day 175

"The bad news is time flies. The good news is you're the pilot."

—Michael Altshuler

In other words, you are in charge of what happens in your life! If you exert your time and energy in pursuit of your dreams and goals, then you will accomplish something worthwhile. Conversely, if you sit on your behind and watch football or game shows for long hours, you will accomplish nothing.

Get up and find something productive to do. Fly your ship productively. Use time wisely to produce a future and to create value from your dreams!

Day 176

"Whatever you do, do with all your might."

—Marcus Tullius Cicero

Don't approach things with a lackluster attitude! Whatever you intend to do—cutting the grass, washing dishes, working on your goals, or working a job—do it with all your attention and effort. It's a habit that will bring you great success. It will first of all allow you to get things done in a powerful way and in good time. But it will also inspire others who are around you and will impress your bosses at work. It will give you a sense of urgency and satisfaction and will make you focus on what you are doing, regardless of the task.

Good habits lead to good work, and that leads to good results!

Day 177

"It's only after you've stepped outside your comfort zone that you begin to change, grow, and transform."

—Roy T. Bennett

It's only when you step out of your particular comfort zone that you really challenge yourself. As long as you are in your comfort zone, there is no real challenge because you are confident you can handle whatever you face. But when you step out of that zone, you will face challenges that you are not confident of, and you will have to think of new solutions and test new skills. Then, you will find out what you are truly capable of and how you will handle failures.

In any situation, profession, or even hobby, you must step out of your comfort zone to improve. If you play golf and play well at a given course, then go to a harder course and play, and even play from the tougher tee positions. Doing so will stretch your skills and make you test your abilities. You will find where your weaknesses lie and what you need to work on. This applies to all areas of life. And after you become accustomed to trying it, it's exhilarating to feel the new challenges!

Day 178

"Do what you love, love what you do, and with all your heart, give yourself to it."

—Roy T. Bennett

When you love what you do, you never work a day in your life! I had a profession that I loved, and I looked forward to getting up and going to it, wanted to stay late, missed it on weekends, and sometimes didn't take vacations. It was almost a hindrance to my marriage. But my wife understood, to a degree, how much I loved it, and she didn't complain. Unfortunately, I had to leave it sooner than I wanted, and I have never really had another profession like it.

Trust me: if you can find a "job" like that, you will be happy to get up and go to it every day! Believe it or not, mine was the Army. I think I was born to be an infantry soldier, and when I had to retire, it broke my heart. Some hated the Army, but to me, it was a dream job.

I truly hope you can find your dream job!

Part II: Days 101–200

Day 179

"If you have a strong purpose in life, you don't have to be pushed. Your passion will drive you there."

—Roy T. Bennett

Our oldest grandson's wife had a desire to be a photographer. At the time, they were young and just starting out, and buying a good camera was a major expense. My wife and I had a good camera, and we were planning on buying a newer one, so we gave our old one to my grandson's wife. It was a good starter camera for her to hone her skills with.

My grandson and his wife were in the Air Force and on the way to their next assignment at that time. When they got there, she practiced and studied photography, and then she started advertising to do free photo shoots for families in the area. All she asked was for them to pay her expenses for the shoot—nothing more. Soon, she was swamped with work and learning new ways to create great pictures.

After a year or so, she started charging a token fee and has upgraded her equipment many times and has added props and items to enhance her photo shoots. That free camera allowed her to pursue her passion, and now she is one of the best photographers I know and is sought after by people of all walks of life. Our gift wasn't responsible for that; it was just a tool in her hands.

You take what you have and use it, practice it, and perfect it. Like our grandson's wife, you become the best you can be with what you have. The camera wasn't the gift; she is! And her passion is still driving her.

Day 180

"Attitude is a little thing that makes a big difference."
—Winston S. Churchill

Your attitude is all that you have, and it will be the make it or break it in your life. With a poor attitude, you will see things in a negative light and lose interest quickly. Blame will be a big part of your personality, and you will fail to learn from your failures. But with a *positive* attitude, you will see good things in life and be motivated to continue in the tough times. You will learn from failure and look forward to getting back up and starting again!

Work on keeping a positive attitude, even when the darkest days are upon you. Remember your past successes and keep positive sayings at hand to remotivate yourself. If nothing else, remember the saying that it's darkest before the dawn!

Day 181

"The man who acquires the ability to take full possession of his own mind may take possession of anything else to which he is justly entitled."

—Andrew Carnegie

Your mind is your key to the universe! You and you alone can control your mind. But all too often, we allow outside things to distract us, and our mind wanders.

You must learn to take possession of your mind and control where it is focused and on what it is focused. Once you do, there is no limit to what you can achieve. The great ones have learned to take possession of their minds so that they can achieve their dreams and goals.

Day 182

"There are no limitations to the mind except those that we acknowledge."

—Napoleon Hill

The boundaries of a nation are set by geography. The boundaries of an event are set by time. The boundaries of your mind are only set by your own limitations!

H. G. Wells lived in the 1800s, long before flight or space travel, but he traveled through time and space in his mind. Jules Verne also lived before those things, but he traveled through space and time in his mind as well. Leonardo da Vinci lived in the 1500s, but he envisioned air travel and things no other man could imagine. He even drew a diagram of a helicopter-style aircraft when flight was unheard of!

Your mind is only limited by your imagination. How far does your mind go?

Part II: Days 101–200

Day 183

"'Knowledge is power.' It is nothing of the sort! Knowledge is only potential power. It becomes power only when, and if, it is organized into definite plans of action and directed to a definite end."

—Napoleon Hill

How true! Knowledge is useless if not put to use properly!

I know numerous people with college degrees in multiple fields who have great knowledge in their chosen fields but can't or won't put that knowledge to work. I call them educated idiots. A total waste of education! They can sit and carry on discussions for hours about their chosen field but produce nothing of value in that field. Total wastes of time and money!

Knowledge should be used to produce something of value, not to produce a smug, self-centered little twerp. Use your knowledge to pursue and accomplish your dream!

Day 184

"I am enough of an artist to draw freely upon my imagination. Imagination is more important than knowledge. Knowledge is limited. Imagination encircles the world."

—Albert Einstein

Einstein was a great genius, but genius was only part of why he discovered all he discovered. Imagination and a desire to explore new things and find out why played parts, too. His desire to know why the universe is, what it is, and how it works is what made him great.

Imagination is the true root of genius, and specifically, the imagination to see that there is something more than the obvious—the imagination to believe in miracles and the unimaginable. That's what drives real genius! That's what creates computers and TVs and smartphones and airplanes . . . *imagination*!

Walt Disney had the gift of imagination, and he created the impossible from nothing and still entertains people seventy-five years later. Use *your* imagination and create *your* dream from nothing!

Part II: Days 101–200

Day 185

"Be the change that you wish to see in the world."

—Mahatma Gandhi

Simple idea and simple act! *Be* the change you want to see!

Don't wait for someone else to do it; *you* do it. You want a new way to do something? Then, create it! You want a new app to do something? Then, create it! You want a new device to do something? Then, make it! People around you are not friendly enough? Then, *you* start being friendlier! *You* must be the change or create the change. Do it!

We always want someone else to take the first step. Well, how about *you* take it for once? *You* be the change and set the pace for others!

Day 186

"Success is not final, and failure is not fatal: it is the courage to continue that counts."

—Winston S. Churchill

Pay attention to this one. Many times in this book, we have focused on not letting failure stop you. But there is a point here that we need to emphasize, which is that success is not final either!

When you achieve success and reach your goal, and your dream is accomplished, that is not the time to sit down and quit. That's the time to reload, get a new vision, a new dream, or a new goal, and start a fresh pursuit.

Look at every great person in history, and you will see that unless they spent their lifetime building one empire, they built several. Rockefeller did more than Standard Oil. JP Morgan did more than Banking. Each one built multiple empires.

Once you succeed, reload and start again! Life goes on, and so should you.

Day 187

"I can't give you a sure-fire formula for success, but I can give you a formula for failure: try to please everybody all the time."

—Herbert Bayard Swope

There's only one person you should try to please, and that is you! I know that if you are married, you will try to please your spouse and your kids and so on. But in reality, in pursuit of your dreams, you have to focus on pleasing you and you alone.

You will need to have an understanding with your spouse and immediate family that your dream is their future too. Their support is essential, and at times, they might be inconvenienced by it. But if they love and support you, then they will ultimately understand. And when you reach your goal, they will reap the rewards too. If they get in on your dream with you, then so much the better!

As for those outside of your immediate circle, though, do not let them influence you with their opinions or try to make you please their needs. You can't please everyone!

Day 188

"Success is not how high you have climbed but how you make a positive difference to the world."

—Roy T. Bennett

All too often, we gauge our success—and others gauge it too—by our position in life. So and so is the CEO, and you are just the Junior VP. So and so is the nephew of the chairman of the board despite not being able to even spell CEO, but you, on the other hand, landed the biggest deal in the corporation's history and saved it from total bankruptcy. So, who is the real success here: you or the person with the fancy title?

History and the facts reveal who is the real success in any given situation, and discerning people realize the truth. Do what you know is best and let the chips fall where they may!

Part II: Days 101–200

Day 189

"The way to get started is to quit talking and begin doing."

—Walt Disney

So many great ideas never get anywhere because they are talked about but never done. An old buddy of mine had a term for what happens when you spend too much time talking about a thing; he called it "paralysis by analysis." We sit around and analyze the situation so long that nothing actually gets done about it.

It is better to start unprepared than never start at all!

Day 190

"Our greatest glory is not in ever falling but in rising every time we fall."

—Oliver Goldsmith

Failure is almost inevitable if you are pursuing something that has never been done! If a person has never failed, then they have never learned, and they have never been tested.

When I worked at the post office, one requirement in the position I was in was the ability to learn routes of mail carriers. You had to test on the routes after studying them, and if you failed any route test three times, you were terminated. One person training for the job had never been fired before, and when they failed a certain route test twice, they just turned in their papers and quit. Several of us tried to encourage the person to at least try the third time, but they said they could not face being fired and would rather quit.

That person quit because they could not risk falling or else, in their mind, they could never get up from that fall. The sad thing was that, just before quitting, the person had taken a trial test and had passed with a high score and probably would have passed the last test too. And that would have been the last route test they would have been given! They just couldn't get past the earlier falls and risk another one.

Part II: Days 101–200

Day 191

"All you need in this life is ignorance and confidence; then success is sure."

—Mark Twain

Sometimes, this is so true! Not knowing you can fail and being so sure you can do something is a sure path to success. Most people fail because they listen to what the "experts" say.

I have said it earlier in this book that when people have told me I can't do something—meaning I am not capable of doing it—I always take that as a challenge and ensure I get it done. As a high school dropout from a single-parent (mother) home with a juvenile criminal record, when I joined the Army, I was not supposed to become an officer. However, in six years and seven months, I reached the rank of Staff Sergeant (E-6), completed a tour in Germany and in Vietnam, was an instructor at Fort Benning, and attended Infantry Officer Candidate School, graduating number one in my class! Not only that, I was handpicked for an assignment in the 3rd infantry, which is The Old Guard in Washington DC—the nation's Honor Guard. Not bad for someone who was repeatedly told he couldn't do it, right?

Don't let anyone tell you that you can't do something!

Day 192

"A thinker sees his own actions as experiments and questions—as attempts to find out something. Success and failure are for him answers above all."

—Friedrich Nietzsche

As you delve deeper into your pursuit and get more accustomed to the pattern of failure and success leading to progress, you get mesmerized by the interaction of the failure and success. A real thinker can become enthralled with the pattern and enjoy the research side as much or more as the progress side. But you have to be careful not to get lost in the intellectual exploration side of things and forget that you are seeking the realization of the dream—the actual accomplishment of the goal!

The hypotheticals can be fascinating. But the end result is what you seek!

Day 193

"It had long since come to my attention that people of accomplishment rarely sat back and let things happen to them. They went out and happened to things."

—Leonardo da Vinci

Take some time and research da Vinci for yourself. Most people know very little about the man. Everyone thinks he was a great scholar and member of the elite from the renaissance era, but nothing could be further from the truth. He was reportedly an illegitimate child and unschooled. He was apprenticed and learned most of what he knew about arts and sciences from working. He apparently was a great genius, but he learned on his own. And like most great geniuses, he had a great imagination that he used to create his great works.

Like da Vinci's quote says, he didn't wait for life to happen to him; he went out and happened to life! Follow his lead, and *you* happen to life!

Day 194

"Success is most often achieved by those who don't know that failure is inevitable."

—Coco Chanel

Blind belief in what you dare to achieve is essential in accomplishing the unique and new! People who create new inventions or business ideas often do it with childlike innocence and belief.

Amazon was created with a daring and faith that an idea ahead of its time would work. FedEx was created as a term paper and given a failing grade, but when put into action in the real world, it passed with flying colors. Mary Kay started a business that no one believed would succeed, but she not only grew rich, she made thousands of ordinary women and men wealthy with her idea.

You might hold the key to another extraordinary idea or product!

Part II: Days 101–200

Day 195

"Kites rise highest against the wind, not with it."

—Winston S. Churchill

Resistance will create the greatest success. Just as a kite rises highest against the wind, trees grow strongest and with the deepest roots when the winds blow hardest.

Your persistence and determination against the resistance of the world to stop your dream will make your work more dedicated, stronger, and more efficient. Anything that is too easy will not be as thorough as what has been accomplished in difficulty! The airplane didn't just work the first time, and neither did the light bulb or the telephone. Great inventions take work and face many failures before they are successful.

Persevere!

Day 196

"The difference between a successful person and others is not a lack of strength, not a lack of knowledge, but rather a lack of will."

—Vince Lombardi

Lombardi was one of the most successful football coaches of all time because he motivated players to be their best. He knew that an average player motivated to give his best was superior to a great player giving a mediocre performance. He also knew that players tended to get slack and rely on "tricks" rather than fundamentals. So, every year, when the season started, Lombardi went back to basics and retrained his team on the basics of football to eliminate the errors they had developed during the season. In his book *Instant Replay*, Jerry Kramer related that Lombardi, at the start of training one year, held up a football in front of the first super bowl champion Green Bay Packers and said, "Gentlemen, this is a football."

Make sure you have the basics and the will to use them!

Part II: Days 101–200

Day 197

"Eighty percent of success is showing up."

—Woody Allen

Wow! What a simple statement. But it is a standard that so many people fail!

People fail to show up for their appointments, their jobs, and even their destinies. You must show up for what you have to do. Show up for school, for work, for meetings, for dates, for assignments, and for anything you are committed to. Don't be unreliable in your life!

Trustworthy people show up and show up on time. Lombardi used to say that if you weren't fifteen minutes early, you were late. It was called "Lombardi time." If you are always rushing to get somewhere and fretting about traffic, you aren't leaving early enough. Plan ahead and get there on time. Better early than late!

Day 198

"Success does not consist in never making mistakes but in never making the same one a second time."

—George Bernard Shaw

Yes! Or, in the words of a well-known proverb: "Fool me once, shame on you. Fool me twice, shame on me!" Making the same mistake twice is inexcusable and completely foolish and a total waste of time and assets. Failure is a great teacher, but as a pastor of mine was fond of saying, "There is nothing to be learned from the second kick of a mule!"

Learn everything from the first failure, and don't repeat it!

Day 199

"You're not obligated to win. You're obligated to keep trying. Do the best you can do every day."

—Jason Mraz

Try, try again! If you keep trying every day and do your best every day, then you have nothing to be ashamed of. Nothing! That is all I or anyone can ask of you or themselves.

Too many people think you have to win at everything to succeed. But winning will not always happen! If it does, that is great. But it won't always. If you give it your best every time, then you have done your best, and you can hold your head high!

If you don't quit, then you are already a winner!

Day 200

"Don't confuse poor decision-making with destiny. Own your mistakes. It's ok; we all make them. Learn from them so they can empower you!"

—Steve Maraboli

The world is full of excuse-makers and blame-shifters—people who don't take responsibility for their poor decisions or mistakes. The sad part is that they don't learn or benefit from what they did! Granted some mistakes can be very costly—even costing lives—but shifting blame doesn't change facts.

When you make a mistake, own it, accept it, analyze it, understand it, learn from it, and then . . . move on! The person who uses mistakes as a learning point will be the strong leader of the future.

PART III

~DAYS 201–300~

Day 201

"If you have a dream, don't just sit there. Gather courage to believe that you can succeed and leave no stone unturned to make it a reality."

—Dr. Roopleen

If you have made it this far in this book and in this year, then by now, you should know that *action* is the key! Positive thinking is great, but without positive action, it is just fantasy. If you have a dream, then you have an obligation to yourself, to your family, and to the world to pursue that dream with all your might—to make that dream a reality.

Dreams are visions of what can be, what should be, and what you are destined to create. Stop procrastinating and go for it!

Day 202

"Problems are not stop signs; they are guidelines!"

—Robert Schuller

Too often, when we are pursuing an issue—especially a difficult one—we use a problem as an excuse to cease work. It's easy to say, "Well, that's the end of that; it can't be done." While a problem might be a good time to stop, step back, and re-evaluate our progress or direction, it is never time to just stop outright!

Problems are simply signs we are doing something wrong—not necessarily a major error, just wrong. If a project involves an electric circuit, we might be overloading part of the system or not applying enough power. Sometimes, problems can be small errors like that and simply need a little fine-tuning.

Edison's experiments with light filaments weren't major errors. Instead, they were just little things that needed adjusting and modifying until the right combination of filament material and vacuum were reached.

Part III: Days 201–300

Day 203

"The universe doesn't give you what you ask for with your thoughts—it gives you what you demand with your actions."

—Steve Maraboli

"I think, therefore I am!" That is a nice philosophy, but it is a lousy way of life!

A frog thinks, a snail thinks, and a dog thinks, but they don't dream and create. *You* are a human being. And when you think, you can dream. And when you dream, you are supposed to take action! *Action* is what sparks things in this universe.

Planets don't sit still in space; they revolve around a star. Galaxies don't sit still; they travel through space. All things in the universe take action. *Actions* are what the universe responds to!

Do something! Even if what you do ends up being wrong, you will get a response, and you can adjust from there.

Day 204

"Rich people have small TVs and big libraries, and poor people have small libraries and big TVs."

—Zig Ziglar

Sometimes, we spend our lives glued to the TV, thinking that we are expanding our minds when in fact, we are feeding it mush! Open a book and use your mind. Your imagination takes the written word and creates whole worlds of places and people. TV shows tell you what to see, where to go, and who is doing something. But books let *you* script and place the action! And your script will always be better than the TV version.

Books also give you knowledge and information upon which you can build and expand your dreams. You can't go everywhere or live in all times, but you can read books by people who have been to those places or lived in those times. Use the experiences of other people to your advantage!

Day 205

"Success is a state of mind. If you want success, start thinking of yourself as a success."
—Joyce Brothers

Yes! Yes! Yes! How you think is directly related to how you are and how others see you! If you think of yourself as a success, then you start acting successful, and your confidence increases, and you *become* successful.

I told you earlier about me becoming an officer in the Army despite my less opportune background. I have never approached any application or interview as if I wasn't qualified or worthy. Instead, I came in like I was the best choice, and I was always *prepared*!

Read, study, and prepare yourself, and you *will* be a success! When I went up before the board of officers to be selected for Officer School, I had already taken the course by correspondence and passed, and so I knew all the answers. Whatever they asked, I was ready for. I was thinking like a success before and as I went in!

Day 206

"Winners are not afraid of losing. But losers are. Failure is part of the process of success. People who avoid failure also avoid success."
—Robert T. Kiyosaki

This is always apparent in places like Vegas. Gamblers who gamble for a living are not afraid of losing a bet; they know it is inevitable in gambling. But they also know that to win, they have to risk losing! Non-gamblers are afraid of losing and will bet fearfully, ultimately losing even what they occasionally win.

That same concept applies in business and to people trying to pursue their dreams. If you are afraid of losing, then you likely will. If you are not afraid of losing—knowing that risk is part of reward—then ultimately, you will win! It's a paradox but true.

You must be willing to face failure if you want to be a winner!

Day 207

"My past has not defined me, destroyed me, deterred me, or defeated me; it has only strengthened me."

—Steve Maraboli

All the trials and troubles you have faced in your past should have made you stronger and better prepared to face your future. The past is gone but has provided you with lessons. And the present is now, when you use those lessons to create your future and pursue your dream. Your future will be what you make it by the choices you make in all your presents to come!

Use your days wisely and your lessons learned judiciously. Your future is in your hands!

Day 208

"If you care about what you do and work hard at it, there isn't anything you can't do if you want to."

—Jim Henson

There are two very key and important points here. First, do you really care about what you are doing? Many people think they care, but they don't! They are putting in a halfhearted effort because they think they are supposed to care. Is what you are doing the driving force in your life? Is it the one thing you care about most? Do you really—*really*—care if it is accomplished? Think about it! It is a very important point to understand.

Second, are you willing to work hard? When people start a project, they don't always realize how hard it is going to be. There will be long hours. There might be hard physical work. There might be hard personal or financial sacrifice. You might even have to forego a career you thought you were going to pursue. The choice will be harder than you realized. Are you willing to work hard at pursuing your dream?

Think about these two points before you jump into your dream. These points can make or break how your dream turns out!

Day 209

"People rarely succeed unless they have fun in what they are doing."

—Dale Carnegie

Yesterday, we talked about hard work, and it might have seemed like I was being morbid or gloomy. But you must understand that hard work isn't a bad thing if you are serious about what work you choose. And in the middle of the work and sacrifice and long hours and failures, if you are doing what you want, then you can and must also have fun!

Sound contradictory? It's not! It doesn't matter what work you choose and what or where it takes you, you will always find humor and fun in the midst of the pursuit of your dream!

Even when I was in the middle of combat, we had humorous times. Once, while on patrol, we were pinned down in a rice paddy by Viet Cong machine-gun fire and had to wait for air power to take them out. Someone started telling knock-knock jokes, and soon, we were all telling them and laughing loudly. We were still pinned down, but we were having a ball telling jokes! Before we got the air support, we realized that the enemy was gone, and we were able to move on. The enemy must have heard us laughing and figured we knew that we had something big on the way or we were too crazy to mess with!

There's always humor to be found in what you do!

Day 210

"Failures are the stairs we climb to reach success."

—Roy T. Bennett

Keep repeating this quote. It is important for you to understand that failure is not terminal. Failure is educational and beneficial!

Thomas Edison had hundreds of failures trying to find the right kind of filament for the light bulb, and each failure eliminated a type of filament that was not a good idea. By the time he found the right one, he knew what *wasn't* right, too. Sometimes, knowing what the solution isn't is about as important as finding the solution!

The great one, Zig Ziglar, taught that every no brought you one step closer to a yes. A point I would add is that each no could teach you something else. First, it could teach you what to change in your sales pitch to make it better. Or, second, it could teach you that the person or company you were selling to didn't need what you were selling but did need something else that you could then come back with later.

Everything can be a lesson!

Part III: Days 201–300

Day 211

"Persistence. Perfection. Patience. Power. Prioritize your passion. It keeps you sane."

—Criss Jami

It is very important to prioritize your passion and direct your efforts in an organized matter. It can be way too easy to attack your goals in a random pattern, overenthusiastically, and end up lost in the confusion of wasted efforts. That's why I have emphasized and will continue emphasizing drawing up a plan and following the plan. The plan may be modified as you go, but you need to keep it as the guide. And don't modify it so much that you lose track of your objective!

Plan, plan, plan! It will keep you focused and directed.

Day 212

"You must expect great things of yourself before you can do them."

—Michael Jordan

You are going to have to be your biggest cheerleader! You will be the one who has the greatest expectations of yourself. When things get tough, you can only depend on one person to be there for you, to cheer you on, and to believe in you and your dream, and that person is *you*! Expect greatness of yourself, and you will achieve greatness. No one will rise higher than the goals they set for themselves!

Day 213

"Success comes from the inside out. In order to change what is on the outside, you must first change what is on the inside."

—Idowu Koyenikan

The inner you is what controls—what dictates—what the outer you becomes! When a person decides to lose weight, the inner person visualizes that weight loss and drives the person to achieve the goal. The actual loss is achieved through the mental discipline and self-control of the inner being.

The person who succeeds in any endeavor does it from the inner being, not the outer being—even the great athletes! When Roger Bannister broke the four-minute mile, he didn't do it because of his outer being but because his inner being drove him to succeed where others had failed. His inner being believed it was possible, and he did it.

You have to drive your outer being to achieve what the inner being believes!

Day 214

"Don't let mental blocks control you. Set yourself free. Confront your fear and turn the mental blocks into building blocks."

—Dr. Roopleen

Mental blocks are vicious. Well, not really. But they are hard to overcome because they are yours and inside your mind.

Usually, mental blocks are based on a fear you have, and you have to find out what that fear is based on so that you can clear the block or blocks up. Get them out of your way and get on the path to work so that you can start creating your dream! Build off those fears and use the energy to motivate yourself to greater heights.

Once you get your mind under control and your fears directed to positive energy and effort, you will be a dynamo of activity!

Day 215

"Success is a little like wrestling a gorilla. You don't quit when you're tired. You quit when the gorilla is tired."

—Robert Strauss

Sounds funny, but it is a good point! You have to keep at it until you are the victor. Don't let the project win! It's easy to quit when you are tired, but it is the champions that keep going when they are tired. And they keep going until they have overcome.

Many of the greatest in every area of life have worked beyond their limits to achieve their goals. That is what has set them apart from the average person and what has made them special in history. Many famous people have warts and wrinkles in their personal lives, but they have accomplished something by exhibiting perseverance and dedication to their areas of expertise. I admire their work, even when I cannot admire them!

Stay the course, finish the race, and succeed in your dream!

Day 216

"The money you make is a symbol of the value you create."

—Idowu Koyenikan

Sometimes, we focus only on the money rather than on what it symbolizes. Money for money's sake is a wasted effort! Realizing that the money you get is a symbol of the value you create—the recognition of your contribution and your worth—is what is important. This is why so many people who win lotteries ultimately end up losing everything, because they really don't earn that money, and the money has no value. They didn't contribute anything to get the money, and it doesn't represent their value.

In another facet, when workers resent the owners having money, they lose sight of the fact that the owner invested the time and money to create the business. The owner took the risk and deserves the return. Without them, the workers would have no jobs. To resent the owner is to resent your job!

The money you will make from your dream is a symbol of what you have created. Enjoy it; you earned it!

Day 217

"You may be the only person left who believes in you, but it's enough. It takes just *one star* to pierce a universe of darkness. Never give up."

—Richelle E. Goodrich

Leonardo da Vinci was persecuted, vilified, and looked down on most of his life because he was not of the upper class, and he was uneducated by the standards of his time. Even as he did his greatest works, he was harassed and abused, and he was doubted by most people of his time. Nevertheless, he believed in himself, and he kept on doing what he did, and he was centuries ahead of his time. Most of his contemporaries are not even remembered.

You have a dream, and you might be the only one who believes in it. Don't stop just because no one else has your vision. They are blind to what you see! Because of people who followed their dreams in spite of others, we have airplanes, telephones, computers, smartphones, etc. Who knows what *you* will add to that list!

Day 218

"To dream of success is to set a goal of where you want to be; to wake up, take action, and achieve it is what true success is all about."

—Idowu Koyenikan

I'm not terribly familiar with Idowu Koyenikan, but his quote is right on! Success is exactly what he said. It is not being the CEO or the president or winning an Oscar or the Super Bowl®. Instead, it is doing just what Koyenikan said!

If you have a goal to be the best garbage collector in your town, and you wake up, get a job as a garbage collector, and become the best one in your town, then you are a *success*! That's it, no questions asked. That's . . . it. That's success in a nutshell!

I should have saved this one for last and closed the book with it!

Day 219

"If you're in the luckiest one percent of humanity, you owe it to the rest of humanity to think about the other ninety-nine percent."

—Warren Buffett

We owe it to others to be aware of their situations and help out when we can. I'm not saying we have to support welfare and all that, but there is a time when we should give our time, talent, and even resources to help others.

I am going to express my personal feelings here, which some may disagree with, and that is fine. There's a scripture in the Bible that says: "Don't cast your pearls before swine; they will trample them into the mud." Now, you can argue the interpretation, but my take on it in life is simply the following. I don't give to people who will take it and use it for worthless reasons like drugs or booze, etc. I also don't give to people who will waste it on tattoos and video games etc.

If I am going to take time to invest my money, time, and talents on someone, they had better be someone who will use it to lift themselves up and try to get ahead. If they want to wallow in slop and use my stuff to do it, then I am not giving! You do what you want. But I am investing in those with some type of ambition. Nuff said!

Day 220

"If you believe you can, you might. If you know you can, you will."

—Steve Maraboli

I equate this quote to the "I will try" versus "I will do" mentality. Believing you can is nice. But will you actually get up and do it? *Knowing* you can is taking action and doing it!

Maybe I am not exactly on target, but that's how I see it. My wife has a saying: "I know that I know that I know." When she says that, don't even think about arguing that point with her!

When I know I can do something, I just do it, and don't tell me I can't!

Part III: Days 201–300

Day 221

"Success is . . . knowing your purpose in life, growing to reach your maximum potential, and sowing seeds that benefit others."

—John C. Maxwell

John Maxwell is a great motivational speaker and leader. Many people have benefitted from his teachings, and I can't argue with his point here. I am not sure it is the best definition of success, but it is a good one.

I will strongly agree that you really need to know your purpose in life! That's what I have been promoting all along in this book by saying that you need to recognize your dream and goals. When you pursue those goals, then you will reach your maximum potential and sow seeds.

Well, I guess this is a pretty good definition of success after all!

Day 222

"The test of success is not what you do when you are on top. Success is how high you bounce when you hit the bottom."

—George S. Patton Jr.

Successful people have a resilience that allows them to bounce back from any failure. As I related earlier in this book, when Steve Jobs was fired from Apple—the company he founded—he could have gone home, gotten drunk, and had a lifelong pity party. Instead, he started another company and soon invented the iPhone.

Not long after that, Apple came to Jobs and not only rehired him but put him back in charge of the company for the rest of his life. He didn't flop; he bounced higher than he was before! Many great people in history failed, but in their failure, they bounced back bigger than before.

What you do when you fall (read it as "fail") is the true indicator of whether you are a success or not!

Day 223

"What is considered impossible is someone else's opinion. What is possible is my decision."

—Idowu Koyenikan

I like this because other people are always telling you that your dream is impossible. Why? Because *they* can't do it—or at least they don't believe they can do it. But of course they can't do it; it's not their dream! It's *yours*.

I imagine the Wright brothers had dozens if not hundreds of people on the sidelines cheering for them to fail. I've read that Leonardo da Vinci was constantly persecuted and harassed even as he created some of his greatest work. Why? Jealousy! Most people do not want you to succeed because they think it will make them look bad!

Ignore the naysayers. Your dream is impossible for them, but it *is* possible for *you*. After all, it's *your* dream!

Day 224

"Love yourself. Forgive yourself. Be true to yourself. How you treat yourself sets the standard for how others will treat you."

—Steve Maraboli

Well, maybe not *all* the time, but it sets the standard they should be treating you by. If you are down on yourself, condemning yourself, and treating yourself as unworthy, then others will definitely follow suit. But if you carry yourself with self-respect, pride, and a sense of worthiness, then even your enemies will be put off and will treat you with a certain respect! They will be unsure of who and what you are.

I mentioned earlier that when I joined the Army, I was a high school dropout from a single-parent (mother) home with a juvenile criminal record. By all social standards, I was not the ideal person to become an Army officer. I was also from the projects, so I supposedly didn't have "social graces."

My first officer assignment was to the elite Old Guard, Honor Guard in Washington DC, where most of my fellow officers were either West Point Academy graduates or ROTC officers. We frequently served at the White House and around high-ranking dignitaries! No one in the unit ever questioned my background because I conducted myself with dignity, self-respect, and proper etiquette. They never suspected where I came from. I was treated with as much respect as anyone there.

It's how you conduct yourself that is how people will perceive you!

Day 225

"The world's greatest achievers have been those who have always stayed focused on their goals and have been consistent in their efforts."

—Dr. Roopleen

I have addressed the two points mentioned in this quote several times so far. You must focus like a laser on your dream or goal and be consistent in your efforts to achieve it! Read about the great successes in our history—men like Lincoln, Washington, Rockefeller, Carnegie, Ford, etc. In every case, you will see these two characteristics (focus and consistency in effort) in their personal endeavors, especially their most prominent achievements.

Many of the greats practically gave up their personal lives and families to pursue their calling and were so consistent in their efforts that they could be found just by knowing what they were pursuing. Edison was mostly found in his laboratory. And Lincoln practically lived in his presidential offices.

Focus and consistency are critical—so much so that you might find yourself with your dream on your mind from awakening to going to sleep . . . and maybe even in your dreams!

Day 226

"Lead, follow, or get out of the way!"
—Unknown

In the Army, this was a byword for many of us. Another variation of it is (as spoken by American astronaut Jim Lovell): "There are those who make things happen, there are people who watch things happen, and those who wonder what happened!"

When something has to be done, decide what role you will play. Will you be a leader, taking charge and leading the way? Will you be a follower, helping with anything you can to get the job done? Or will you not be involved at all but also not interfere with those who are working?

Whichever role you choose, it will help get the task done. Too many people choose not to lead and not to follow, but they stand around getting in the way, impeding the work of those who are trying to get something done. It is better to get out of the way and let the others work!

Part III: Days 201–300

Day 227

"Life always begins with one step outside of your comfort zone."

—Shannon L. Alder

In my Army career, I was always meeting people who would say, "I almost went airborne" or "I almost went Special Forces." Or, sadly, some would say, "I almost served in combat."

Now, I am not being dramatic or an elitist, but when they would say these things, I usually smiled and nodded and either didn't reply or made some reassuring comment. But to those of us who *had* done those things, we knew something that set us apart and that applies to today's quote. What we knew is that life—meaning living apart from a mundane reality—came with *actually* doing what these people say they *almost* did!

Stepping out of an airplane at 1,200 feet with a parachute on your back is exhilarating. Life takes on a new meaning, and you are never quite the same. Similarly, going Special Forces puts you through training you will never get anywhere else, and you do things most people will never do. It sets you apart, and life is never the same. (Rangers are like that too.) Being a combat soldier in real combat is something you can never explain, but it makes you see living in a way other people will never see.

When you decide to step out of your comfort zone and pursue your dream, you will experience something akin to those feelings, and you will never see life like others do again. So, do it! Step out of your comfort zone. Feel your hair raise, feel your skin crawl, feel your gut clench, and feel the fear rise up, but all under *your* control. Live life like others never experience!

Day 228

"Don't let what you cannot do interfere with what you can do."

—John R Wooden

There are a lot of things I can do, a lot of things I have learned, and a lot of things I have experienced in my life. But there are a ton of things I just can't do! If I listed all of the things I know I can't do, I would have a trilogy of books for sure. However, for the most part, those things don't stop me from doing something if I can!

Even if there's something I am unsure about, if I have some knowledge about a part of it, I can start it and learn as I go—the old trial and error approach. There is also the fact that, as I go, when I reach an impasse that I can't overcome, there's someone out there who can do what I can't and might be willing to help out! We've talked several times about bringing in others to help—building a team—and this is why. It's because there are things you don't know or can't do. You need other people's skills and knowledge! Even the most brilliant people out there need others, even if for no reason other than that they can conceive everything, but someone else has to fabricate it.

Don't be intimidated by what you can't do. Start with what you *can* do and bring in help as you go!

Part III: Days 201–300

Day 229

"No matter how small you start, always dream big."
—Stephen Richards

Absolutely! Amazon was started in a garage! Think about it; the biggest, most successful online retailer in the world—in history—was started by a few people out of a garage. Don't you think they were thinking big?

There were a lot of people that would have put big money on either Bezos was crazy as a mad hatter, or that he was going to fail miserably, or both. But neither one was the case. He was already planning the system that's out there today. Likewise, Mary Kay started in her home, but she envisioned a makeup empire that spanned the world.

Don't try to grow with a small vision; it doesn't work! Have a *grand* vision—a *worldwide* vision. It is better to shoot for the stars and just hit the moon than shoot for the ceiling and hit it!

Day 230

"Failure should be our teacher, not our undertaker. Failure is delay, not defeat. It is a temporary detour, not a dead-end. Failure is something we can avoid only by saying nothing, doing nothing, and being nothing."

—Denis Waitley

You keep seeing this point because you need it engrained in your mind! Failure is a teaching point. It is, as said earlier in this book, a part of your stairway to success. The only fault in failure is repeating the same failure over and over. Learn from each failure and try again in a new way.

Failure is a necessity for success—*real* success!

Day 231

"The victim mindset dilutes the human potential. By not accepting personal responsibility for our circumstances, we greatly reduce our power to change them."

—Steve Maraboli

This is one of the biggest issues with people today; they want to play the victim! Instead of accepting responsibility, they want to point the finger of blame, thereby not learning from life's lessons and becoming doomed to constantly repeating their errors. By playing the victim, they avoid responsibility and, consequently, avoid opportunity as well.

Decades ago, government interference created a welfare mentality that has created a dependence on society to support and provide for people's needs. This has often removed the desire to work for wages and to succeed beyond basic necessities. Many people have become complacent, and dreams have become nonexistent in their lives!

You must avoid that mentality at all costs. No one owes you anything, and you alone should assume responsibility for your future. When you surrender your care to someone or some entity, you have also surrendered your freedom to them or to it!

Day 232

"Be curious about the world in which you live. Look things up. Chase down every reference. Go deeper than anybody else—that's how you'll get ahead."

—Austin Kleon

As I said before, Leonardo da Vinci was an illegitimate child and did not receive formal schooling. Most of his education in engineering and the arts came from being an apprentice to others in those fields. The one thing he had was a great mind and an even greater curiosity.

Because da Vinci used his great curiosity to look things up—sometimes things others had never studied—and chased down every reference, and because he was willing to explore deeper and more thoroughly than anyone else, he is now considered one of the great geniuses of all time. He dissected cadavers and did drawings of the human anatomy that are still used in the medical field today. And he did so without microscopes or other special instruments! He also drew machinery that was unimagined and ahead of his time by centuries. He drew a machine that is similar to a helicopter!

Da Vinci did all that because he was curious and willing to explore the possibilities!

Day 233

"Who you are tomorrow begins with what you do today."

—Tim Fargo

Your past does not define you now, but what you do today will define who you can be tomorrow! Sound contradictory? Well, if you made mistakes in the past, you are not necessarily a bad person, because you can change! If you want to be or do something different in the future, you can set in motion actions that will make that come to pass.

If you want to be a doctor, you can create that by starting on the path of education that will lead to that profession. If you stick with it, then after a period of dedicated and successful study and work, you will end up a doctor. You want to be a schoolteacher instead? Well, the same rule applies! Want to be a wealthy investor? Begin studying investment strategies and investing in the best investments to produce the wealth you desire. In time, given wise investing, you will reach your goals!

Like each pursuit discussed here, laser focus and dedicated work will be required to achieve *your* dreams and goals.

Day 234

"It is in your moments of decision that your destiny is shaped."

—Anthony Robbins

No matter where you are or where you end up, the sum total of who you are and what you are is always the result of the decisions you make along the way!

The homeless person you see crouched under the bridge in the cold is there often—though certainly not always—because of decisions they made. The prisoner cutting grass along the road is there because of decisions they made. The cashier at the fast-food restaurant is often—though not always—there because of decisions they made. The banker is there because of decisions they made. The CEO of the corporation is there because of decisions they made.

All of these people have one thing in common, which is that their position in life is usually the result of the decisions they made. So, make sure you make wise decisions along the way!

Part III: Days 201–300

Day 235

"Courage is the most important of all the virtues because without courage, you can't practice any other virtue consistently."

—Maya Angelou

Most people, when they think of courage, think of soldiers in battle, or a mountain climber, or some daring adventurer. But courage is found in many more places than those kinds of extreme activities!

Courage is a young pregnant woman, unmarried, deciding to give birth instead of having an abortion and raising the child on her own if need be. *That's* courage! Courage is a father standing up to his boss over a moral issue, knowing he might lose his job and not be able to feed his family or pay the bills but also knowing his character is more important than a paycheck. *That's* courage!

Courage is not just facing physical danger; it is a moral thing, it is an emotional thing, and it is so often unseen and unheralded by the world. Courage is seen in parents, teachers, pastors, average men and women, and little children. When a child faces the bully at school to defend a classmate, *that* is courage!

When you face public or family ridicule to pursue your dream, *THAT* is courage!

Day 236

"Instead of worrying about what you cannot control, shift your energy to what you can create."

—Roy T. Bennett

Worry is always a waste of time. Planning for the future is not a waste of time. But planning against those things you cannot control is as bad a waste of time as worry. So, evaluate what you can control and what you can protect against, and then focus on what you can create.

All the rest is out of your control, and concerning yourself with it is wasted time and energy! Let those who can control it be concerned with taking action. I'm not saying don't be concerned. But do not waste time fretting over what you cannot influence.

You have to focus on your dreams and goals and ensure they are taken care of!

Part III: Days 201–300

Day 237

"Make improvements, not excuses. Seek respect, not attention."

—Roy T. Bennett

As you progress in life, look for ways to improve yourself and your work. If you fail, don't make excuses. Instead, learn from the failures and improve your efforts. Wise men and women learn from every experience, good and bad! Foolish people make excuses and blame others when they falter.

Seek to be respectable and reliable in all you do because this will draw others to you to support you and your work. Flashy, attention-seeking shows of action often fail or create illusions that people want to avoid. The most successful people in history were usually low-key and honest in their work, and they drew the support of respected investors.

Day 238

"No matter how much suffering you went through, you never want to let go of those memories."

—Haruki Murakami

The memories of your past and your struggles will keep you humble and grounded as you progress, especially in achieving success. When you forget or closet your past, you might become haughty and overbearing, forgetting that you were once down yourself. Remembering what you have overcome and those who helped along the way will be an encouragement when you face difficulties again down the road. All of our past experiences are meant to strengthen us, not weaken us!

Day 239

"Happiness is not the absence of problems; it's the ability to deal with them."

—Steve Maraboli

Too many people think that the absence of problems will bring happiness. But true happiness is the ability to deal with life's situations as they arise. Life will always have some curveball to throw at you—personal, emotional, financial, etc. Your ability to handle each one will determine your level of happiness!

The more problems you handle, the less they affect you, and the better your life will be on a daily basis. The person who goes along unchallenged and then suddenly faces a disaster is the one who crumbles under pressure. The person who routinely handles stress with a flare will be unfettered by life's glitches—even some of the most serious—because they are practiced at the art of handling situations.

Don't avoid life; face it head-on with anticipation!

Day 240

"Do not lie to yourself. We have to be honest about what we want and take risks rather than lie to ourselves and make excuses to stay in our comfort zone."

—Roy T. Bennett

I have met many people who lie to themselves that they are happy where they are or with what they have when in fact, they hate their lives. In reality, they envy others who have succeeded, but they are unwilling to step out and do what those others have done to achieve a better life. When faced with a situation, they declare it doesn't bother them when, in reality, deep in their gut, it's like a spring tightening and making them sick with anger or tension. But they won't face the reality of dealing with the situation like other people!

Be willing to step out of your comfort zone to do something new, stretch your world, and challenge yourself to resolve issues that are bothering you. Seek your dreams. Your dreams are there for a reason: to make you better!

Part III: Days 201-300

Day 241

"Once you realize you deserve a bright future, letting go of your dark past is the best choice you will ever make."

—Roy T. Bennett

So many people live in the belief that they do not deserve better than they have and that what they have is already more than they deserve. All too often, it is ingrained from childhood that we are worms in the dirt and worthless in society. In other words, that we cannot expect more than hand to mouth, and if we struggle all our lives, we will be lucky to survive to old age.

HOGWASH!

You are entitled to what you are willing to work for and nothing less! The world is your oyster, and there are pearls aplenty to be harvested. Opportunity exists for everyone, in equal measure, if you will just go for it.

The old idea that only the wealthy and elite get a break is wrong! They might get a head start, but they don't have a better chance than you. Sometimes, if you use your street-smarts, you can bypass them and beat them to the finish line.

Rockefeller started out as a poor person, and his father took the meager money he had acquired and left the family to starve. John D. worked hard for someone else and saved his earnings until he saw an opportunity in refining kerosene. Then, with proper planning and wise investing, he quickly rose to become one of the richest men in America!

Look for opportunities, find your niche, and seize the moment!

Day 242

"Hiding how you really feel and trying to make everyone happy doesn't make you nice, it just makes you a liar."

—Jenny O'Connell

Honesty is always the best policy, even if it isn't the best course of action socially! I am not advocating running around being a sourpuss. But don't try to conform to everyone else when you feel another way. They might all be conforming but feeling different and just need a leader to step up and give them an alternative.

As mentioned earlier in this book, I read that at one point in time in the 1770s, only about 13–15 percent of the population of the colonies openly supported the revolution. If the leaders hadn't expressed their real feelings, then nothing would have happened, and we would probably still be a British colony today! But people like Jefferson, Madison, and Washington expressed what they really felt and banded together and gave the populace a rallying point from which to form a fighting force around.

When you are in pursuit of your dreams, many will oppose you and be derogatory about your goals, so you have to be willing to stand up for yourself and state your feelings!

Part III: Days 201–300

Day 243

"Maturity is when you stop complaining and making excuses and start making changes."

—Roy T. Bennett

So very true! As long as all you do is make excuses and complain, you are like a car spinning its wheels—you aren't going anywhere!

Excuses don't allow you to learn from mistakes; they deflect the lessons and blame other people or things. You need to own your mistakes, analyze them, and learn why and how they occurred. Only then can you see how to proceed and avoid them again.

Complaining is a waste of time and effort. Instead, spend that time and energy investigating how to do it better and correctly. People don't like whiners! If you want helpers and investors, they want to be associated with mature, responsible people who can be relied upon.

Grow up, show up, and sometimes, you need to shut up!

Day 244

"Strong people have a strong sense of self-worth and self-awareness; they don't need the approval of others."

—Roy T. Bennett

When you achieve a positive self-image and a strong sense of self-worth and self-awareness, you are not concerned with the approval of others! That doesn't mean you don't care about other people. To the contrary, you actually begin to care a great deal about others; you just aren't seeking their approval.

You know what you are doing, where you are headed, and what you want in life. What other people think about your goals and pursuits is not important in your decision-making process. You find yourself associating mainly with those people of like-minded goals, aspirations, and beliefs and avoiding negative people.

If and when you need help, you seek it from those who you know are either supportive of your ideas or are open to new ideas. In short order, your circle of associates becomes smaller and tighter and more specialized out of natural selection. It is not because you are a snob but rather because you don't have time to waste on distractions. It doesn't make you less of a person but rather allows you to focus on your dreams and dedicate your efforts to accomplishing your goals.

Day 245

"Two things are infinite: the universe and human stupidity, and I'm not sure about the universe."

—Albert Einstein

Einstein fascinates me because, for all his genius, he was a normal human being with wit and a sense of sarcasm. I think I would have loved being around him on a personal level. Though, for the most part, when he started his scientific talk, I would not have understood a thing he said! Einstein wasn't stuffy and dry, but he was capable of switching to an amazing intellectual level, and he could then switch back to a totally human perspective.

Humor is not for everyone, but to me, real genius includes a sense of humor and what I call a sense of nonsense. It is not rude or crude to make humorous observations. They are realistic observations of life! We, as a species, can do some of the dumbest things imaginable. Some are done innocently, and in that vein, humorously. Others are done in seriousness and are scary when done by so-called leaders or people of authority.

I like my friend's definition of "expert" that I told you earlier in this book: "Ex" = has been, and "Spurt" = drip under pressure. In other words, many so-called experts know absolutely nothing!

Day 246

"You do not write your life with words . . . You write it with actions. What you think is not important. It is only important what you *do*."

—Patrick Ness

Ah, the ones who can talk a good game but do nothing! The great advisors who sit on the sidelines and tell others what and how to do it but have yet to ever do a thing! They are everywhere. As a buddy of mine liked to say, "Never let anyone who has done nothing tell you how to do anything."

The results you achieve and the legacy you leave will not be based on your words—unless you are an author—but on the results of your actions! If Ford had talked about his automobiles and his assembly line ideas his whole life but did nothing about it, no one would remember him today. I am sure there were many people who talked about ideas for cars and manufacturing but never did anything. He *did* something, and he became a household name, even if you don't like Fords.

Carnegie didn't just talk about how to manufacture steel. Instead, he set about actually building factories to manufacture steel and sell it. In doing so, he became the richest man in America! There were probably many people who talked about steel but did nothing. They are unknown today.

Don't just think about it, and don't just talk about it. Get up off your couch and *do* something about it!

Day 247

"Without deviation from the norm, progress is not possible."

—Frank Zappa

If you aren't familiar with Frank Zappa, look him up! Read about his life and style, and you will find out that this was more than just a quote. And the quote is accurate for everyone.

If no one ever deviated from the norm, we would still be carrying wooden clubs, living in caves, and hunting mastodons . . . or something of that nature. Every advance in any aspect of our life—technological, industrial, agricultural, sociological, etc.—comes about as a deviation from the norm!

The car was a deviation from the norm of walking and of horse and buggy. The industrial age was a deviation from the agricultural age. The technological age is a deviation from the industrial age. Television was a deviation from radio. And on and on . . .

Each step in our advancement was a deviation from the norm. So, don't think your ideas are weird, and don't let others make you think they are. The deviation is necessary!

Day 248

"Do not fear to be eccentric in opinion, for every opinion now accepted was once eccentric."

—Bertrand Russell

"That's weird. You're crazy. Man will *never* fly!" said many, many people to the Wright brothers. "You are insane. You can't send sounds across the ocean without wires!" they said to Marconi. "Man will never walk on the moon! It's impossible to pass through the Van Allen belts and live!" they said about the space program. And probably at some point, long, long ago: "A wheel? That thing will *never* work. What good is a wheel?!"

All through time, new ideas and inventions have been declared eccentric or impossible, but today, we accept them as routine! At one point, they said the sun revolved around Earth, not Earth around the sun. It was even said that Earth is flat and held on the back of a giant tortoise. (Yes, people really believed that!)

Your dream might be declared crazy and impossible today, but after you create it, people will claim they knew it would work all along!

Day 249

"The past has no power over the present moment."
—Eckhart Tolle

No matter what you are talking about, the past has no real power over the present! Unless . . . you give it power.

If you messed up in the past, and you let that past impact your present and hold you back, then you have given it power. But the beauty is that you can let go of your past and take control of your present and start a new day in your life. Similarly, if your dream has been tried in the past and failed, that doesn't mean it's not valid to try again now. First off, the person who tried before might have given up too soon or taken a wrong approach. Or maybe it was the wrong time, and the technology wasn't supportive.

For example, imagine if you were born in 1866 and you had the dream of a smartphone. It would have been technologically impossible to build because all the components and supporting systems were nonexistent. There wasn't even a functional telephone yet! So, ideas and timing are relevant.

As mentioned earlier in this book, da Vinci drew a flying machine similar to a helicopter. But there were no motors to drive it, and hand-cranked rotors would hardly generate sufficient lift. It was an idea ahead of its time.

Dare to try *your* dream!

Day 250

"The reasonable man adapts himself to the world; the unreasonable one persists in trying to adapt the world to himself. Therefore, all progress depends on the unreasonable man."

—George Bernard Shaw

Therein lies the crux of the situation. Man's future lies in the hands of what most of society considers the nutty professor!

The people who will set the future are the ones who are dissatisfied with the present and are willing to step out of their comfort zones to seek their visions, their dreams. They are positive, motivated, and focused on a vision that they alone can see. These "crazies" will create tomorrow's world!

We dream-seekers are not really crazies; we are adventurers. Like Davy Crockett and Daniel Boone, we are exploring the vast frontier. They had unknown wilderness; we have unknown science and technology (or whatever area your dream is in).

We dream-seekers aren't unruly, but we aren't satisfied with the "norm" or the pat answer. We are the kid who always asked, "Why?" And, after the long and arduous answer we were given, we said, "Why?" again, much to our teacher's or parent's frustration. The only person who could ever answer us adequately was another person like us because they knew we weren't looking for the schoolbook answer; we were looking deeper!

"WHY?!"

Day 251

"Do not train a child to learn by force or harshness but direct them to it by what amuses their minds so that you may be better able to discover with accuracy the peculiar bent of the genius of each."

—Plato

Forcing a child, or anyone, to learn something deprives them of the freedom to explore their personal interests and natural desires. When I was young, I liked science and history, and I had a natural gift at basic math. But had someone forced me into studying math and advanced mathematics because of my "gift," I would have rebelled and would not have been most effective since science and history were my greatest interests.

I never advanced much past basic algebra. But I did fare well in studying sciences and all of history. Had I stayed in education as a career, I believe I would have been a history teacher, researcher, or possibly an archeologist.

When my grandson came to me stating that he wanted to go into the military, he expected me to encourage him to go Army since I am a retired Army officer. Instead, I suggested he try the Air Force because his real interests in life are in computers, and I know the Air Force offers the best opportunities in that area. He is doing great and making a successful career in the Air Force because he is where he can grow!

Are You Positive?

Day 252

"It is not true that people stop pursuing dreams because they grow old; they grow old because they stop pursuing dreams."

—Gabriel García Márquez

The day you stop pursuing your dreams is the day you start growing old, even if that day is when you are a teenager! I have seen people lose the flicker of hope and excitement and stop living, and it is a frightening thing to see. It is almost as bad as watching a person physically die. I have seen many people die; it is a side effect of growing older and especially of having been in combat. I have seen life leave the eyes and the face go slack, and in many cases, real death is less disturbing than when you see someone lose hope!

As I have mentioned before in this book, I love the stories of those who kept dreaming and pursuing their dreams and reaching their goals in later years. Harland Sanders at sixty-five-plus years of age with Kentucky Fried Chicken. Grandma Moses, a successful artist in her mid-eighties. And many others in late life as well. Biblically, Moses came back at age eighty to lead the Israelites to freedom. It is never too late to pursue your destiny!

I had a professor who, at age sixty-four, was going for her CPA. It would take almost four years, and her friends and family kept telling her it was a waste of time because, by the time she got it, she would be almost sixty-nine. Her reply was, "Okay, but if I don't do it now, how old will I be in four years?" It was the first time I ever heard that, and it stuck. Do it anyway! You will still be the same age in whatever number of years from now, so at least have something to show for your time.

Day 253

"The important thing is not to stop questioning. Curiosity has its own reason for existing."

—Albert Einstein

Leonardo da Vinci is a classic example of this! He explored everything—not just art but science, medicine, and just about everything that piqued his curiosity. As a result, he gained knowledge that even the most educated people of his time did not have.

Da Vinci's curiosity, combined with his imagination, caused him to create drawings of his imagined ideas that actually exist today. His drawings showed imagined aircraft, war machines, and other items that were centuries ahead of their time. The only reason he couldn't build them was that there was no industrial or technological system to provide the materials he needed. His anatomical sketches are so accurate that it's as if he had CAT scans to break down the cadavers he examined. Many of his works are still used today!

Question everything. No matter how many experts say it is so, check to see if they have explored every aspect. We are always getting new insight or corrections on old facts. I recently read somewhere that they are even correcting Einstein's theory of relativity!

Day 254

"The merit of all things lies in their difficulty."

—Alexandre Dumas

There's an old saying: "If it were easy, everyone would be doing it." That is so true! Sometimes, the only reason it hasn't been done is because it is difficult! Breaking the four-minute mile in running just required a little extra mental effort; the physical ability was there all along. Runners were right on the cusp of doing it, but psychologically, it was too difficult. As mentioned earlier in this book, when Roger Bannister finally broke the four-minute mile, within a few weeks, numerous other runners did it too. Why? Now, it was no longer difficult!

When Tiger Woods began playing on the PGA tour, he struck awe not only in fans but in other players as well. But after a few years, it seemed Tiger was losing it. The fact is, he was still just as good, but the other players and new players realized that what he was doing they could do too. So, the game moved to a new level!

You might be the one who has to do what others see as too difficult. Set the new standard and be the leader! Follow your dream, set your goal, and don't be afraid to put in the work, be it physical work, mental work, or just time. It *will* pay off!

Day 255

"The most important thing is this: to sacrifice what you are now for what you can become tomorrow."

—Shannon Alder

There's a saying: "Short-term sacrifices for long-term gains." This is usually the key to achieving your dreams and accomplishing your goals.

Investors realize that putting money into any investment is a long-term thing, and they are surrendering the use of that money for things they could have now for the returns they will get later. Going to the gym to work out is an example. You work out daily, giving up time and energy for the body and health you want down the road. Same with your education.

The key is pursuing your dream! You must surrender time, social life, and other things to pursue the dream. When you sit back and watch Tom Hanks in a movie and marvel at what a great actor he is, remember that he wasn't born a great actor. Instead, he has worked his whole life and is still working at his craft. When you watch that athlete doing their sport with almost mechanical precision, it's not because they are a natural, it is because they have been working at it most of their lives and still do every day.

You must be willing to give up something now for what you will be tomorrow!

Day 256

> "Successful people enjoy the journeys they embark on, irrespective of whether they reach their destination or not."
>
> —Zain Hashmi

This might seem like a copout, but it's not. There is no guarantee you will ever achieve your dream. Not all people do!

One of the greatest geniuses of our time—the creator of some things we use today and ideas we have built on in modern times—never actually reached the dream he had. He left behind a legacy, but for decades, his name was almost unknown to people. Once, when asked what it felt like to be the smartest man alive, Einstein said, "I don't know, ask _____," referring to this man. Can you guess who it was?

It was Nikola Tesla! He is widely believed to be the greatest genius of the last century and possibly all time. He created alternating current (AC) and the system to produce it while working for Thomas Edison and was fired by Edison. His electric motor is the basis for the motor in the Tesla automobile, ergo the name of the car. And there are so many other devices based on his work that it is hard to imagine where we would be without him and his work. And yet, he died penniless and without having achieved his dream!

Tesla's dream was to use Earth as a natural source to create a system to broadcast electric power through the air to people around the world and to do it for free. He came close, but his sponsors withdrew their backing for fear that the experiment might work!

Day 257

"Doing the tough things sets winners apart from losers."

—Stephen Richards

This is so true! It doesn't matter what field of endeavor you pursue; this is the fine line that separates the cream from the milk.

Why was Michael Jordan the greatest? Because he worked the hardest and the longest and saw his own weaknesses and corrected them. The tough thing!

Why did Dr. Ben Carson rise from a single-parent family in the projects to become one of the nation's leading neurosurgeons and later get appointed to a presidential cabinet post? Because he was willing to sacrifice his social life, dedicate his time to his work, and do the tough things to achieve his goals and become a success!

How did Jeff Bezos develop a small garage mail-order business into the largest online merchandizing business in the world in just a few decades? He was willing to make the tough choices, make the sacrifices, and do what others weren't doing!

Are you willing to make the tough choices, do the tough things, and give up things to achieve *your* dreams?

Day 258

"People are successful because they think and act like successful people."

—Roy T. Bennett

"This is repetitious. We've discussed this before!" you say. Yes, it is! And that's the point. When you go to the gym, do you do one sit up and say, "Okay, that's my ab workout for life"? No, you do repetitions, and you do them every time you go. Repetition pays off physically and mentally. The purpose of this book is to help you reprogram your thinking and attitude. So, in many ways, we have to repeat the positive input—maybe not the exact words but the same ideas.

How you think affects how you act, and how you act affects how you are received, and how you are received is how people react to you, and how people react to you affects how you think about yourself. It is one big circle, and it all serves to reinforce your self-image!

There is a thing called self-talk. Literally, it is talking to yourself—like lecturing yourself. It is proven that the most important words you hear are those you speak to yourself. If you say things like, "I'm stupid" or "I can't get anything right," you will believe yourself. So, stop self-talking in negative terms! *STOP IT!*

Self-talk in positive and uplifting ways. Tell yourself you can, you are smart, you know things, you are successful, etc. If you are going in to meet with someone on a matter, have the meeting with yourself first, and discuss every aspect you can, prepare your answers, research the matter, and be the expert. When you go into the actual meeting, be confident, and if they hit you with something you aren't prepared for, don't panic or stammer. Instead, just say something like, "I'm sorry, I'm not sure on that matter, but I would like to research it and get back to you if I may?" They will see you as professional, and if it's an important matter, they will say, "Fine."

Act successful!

Day 259

"The line between failure and success is so fine . . . that we are often on the line and do not know it."

—Elbert Hubbard

Simply put, don't assume you've failed just because you haven't obviously succeeded. Edison's lab techs were just one filament away from success before they got the right one! Think how fine a light bulb filament is. They were that close. What if they'd quit?!

Sometimes, the experiment is right, but the stimulus is wrong. Say you used 100 volts. Well, maybe it needs 110 volts! Dreams are tenuous things, and you might not have a clear picture of exactly what you are pursuing. You think you do, but when you get there, you don't actually realize that's it.

I liken it to seeking a dream mate. For me, I am going to say the dream wife. I might have the dream mate in my mind as a five-foot, five-inch blonde with blue eyes. But if I stick with that image, I have eliminated millions of women who might actually be better. If I go out more open-minded, I might find that my real dream mate is a five-foot, two-inch brunette with brown eyes.

Your dream is a guide. As you pursue it, refine it down so that you don't miss it when you get there!

Part III: Days 201–300

Day 260

"You are in danger of living a life so comfortable and soft that you will die without ever realizing your true potential."

—David Goggins

In our day and time, with all our technological toys, this is a real danger! I watch people living on their smartphones, laptops, and televisions. I am guilty of it myself, and that is part of why I am writing this book—to deliver myself from that life!

It is too easy to become a techno potato these days. It has come to the point where we have to force ourselves get up and exercise our bodies, our minds, and our intellect. One thing I do is take daily trivia quizzes. My wife thinks it is silly, but it makes me think in a variety of areas and exercise my mind out of the norm. I also try to engage in some physical exercise—not just conventional but also things like yard work and home remodeling. I have also started writing and have started reading real books.

Technology is great, but we can't become so dependent on it that it becomes our life!

Day 261

> "Never underestimate the power you have to take your life in a new direction."
>
> —Germany Kent

Too many people think that now is too late to change their life. People of all ages feel this way. But the fact is that, at any age, you can change your life's direction!

Remember the list by now? It is famous people like artist Grandma Moses (in her eighties) and Harland Sanders, founder of KFC (in his sixties), who changed their lives at late ages. You can do it at any age if you have the desire! Decide what new path or direction you want to take, what actions you need to pursue them, and then take the actions necessary.

Maybe you studied radiation therapy in college and have worked in that field for twenty years, but now, you decide you want to be an auto mechanic. Go to trade school, learn mechanics, and go for it! As mentioned before, I know a man who had been in computers all his life and was successful at it, but he was miserable in his job. In his middle age, he decided to do what he had always wanted—to be a mechanic. And he did just that. Now, he is happy and enjoys going to work every day!

You can change anytime, for any reason!

Part III: Days 201–300

Day 262

"I was taught to strive not because there were any guarantees of success but because the act of striving is in itself the only way to keep faith with life."

—Madeleine Albright

Sometimes, the act of striving is the pursuit of the dream! Too many people stop striving and start existing, and life ceases for them.

Strive—no matter what it is for, strive! Strive to learn, strive to achieve, and strive to be your best at whatever you do. It gives you a purpose—a sense of being that makes each day special.

Don't feel your lot in life is unimportant. It isn't! Your place is essential in the grand scheme, no matter what the place or scheme is. Every gear on the cog is necessary for the perfect function. If one gear is out of place or inoperative, then the whole machine is not right. *You* are important!

If you have a special dream, pursue it with all your heart and strive to achieve its completion!

Day 263

"Small shifts in your thinking and small changes in your energy can lead to massive alterations of your end result."

—Kevin Michel

When the captain of a large seagoing vessel like a cruise ship wants to change direction, they don't make sudden, sharp changes in course. Instead, they make small, gradual changes that gradually shift the huge vessel toward its new destination. This prevents extreme stresses on the vessel and disruptions to the passengers, and it still brings the vessel to the new course—in a smooth and accurate transition.

When you are changing your life or working on your dream, subtle changes are most effective in altering the end results you desire. If you make changes too fast or too radically, you might not allow yourself and those around you the time to adjust to the new direction and purpose you are seeking. By doing it subtlety and with slow but consistent effort, things progress smoothly and allow for ease of adaptation!

Plan ahead and make changes gradually over time!

Day 264

"There is no try. There is only do."

—John Green

Trying is a weak response; it leaves an open door to failure. Don't just try something. Set out to really and fully do it! Anyone can try, but a winner *does it*. No matter what it takes, a winner gets the job done.

Your mindset has to be, *I will do it, and I can do it!* Then, you are bound and determined to accomplish your task, regardless of the difficulty. An "I'll try" approach leaves you an open door to fail and an excuse of "I can't" or "I couldn't." Instead, have an I can, I will, I am going to do it attitude!

A positive person has the attitude that they can and will accomplish what they set out to do!

Day 265

"Keep dreaming, and with the right habits, dreams can become realities!"

—Larry Biggers

If you have the right habits—the habits of a winner—your dreams will become a reality! Dreams are visions you see that others cannot. You set your dreams as goals and put them in writing as a plan. The plan is phased with time schedules and objectives, and you begin working toward completion. You might adjust your plan as you go based on obstacles or successes you encounter, but you stick with it and stay focused on the end goal like a laser sight!

Persistence and a burning desire to see your dream come to fruition will bring it to pass. The proper work and thought habits will drive you to successful completion. Negativity becomes a thing of the past as you move ever closer to your goals.

Keep the vision before your eyes—write it on tablets, look at it daily, and see it as a reality!

Part III: Days 201–300

Day 266

"Success isn't the result of things you do occasionally but rather the things you do consistently!"

—Unknown

Consistency is the key to accomplishing any objective you have in life! Want to fulfill your dream? Be consistent! Want to have a successful marriage? Be consistent! Want to raise good children? Be consistent! Want to invest and build wealth? Be consistent! Want success? *Be consistent!*

It's all about one word: consistency!

Day 267

"Sometimes, the greatest pleasure in life is doing what other people said you weren't capable of doing!"

—Unknown

I think if I had a catchphrase for my life, especially my early life, this would have been it. As I have said before, in my younger days, it was like a challenge when someone told me I couldn't do something (meaning wasn't capable of doing something). It then became like an obsession for me to get it done! I loved the look on people's faces when I did what they said I couldn't do. And especially so when it was good for me or my career.

Never, ever let someone stop you by saying you are not capable of doing something. I don't care if it has never been done before. *You* be the first!

Day 268

"It isn't where you came from that matters but rather where you are going that matters."

—Anonymous

Oh boy, this is another one I love! People are quick to judge your past or your background and tell you that you don't fit in or don't have what it takes. So many people think that because you aren't from their social group or economic strata or educational background, you aren't fit to be at some level or in some job.

Just remember, again, Leonardo da Vinci: he was a poor, illegitimate, uneducated man serving as an apprentice. BUT he ended up being the real genius of his age—developing the great ideas, writing the great papers, and painting the great paintings. It wasn't where he came from but rather where he was going!

You are the same. Your past doesn't define what your present is or what your future holds. Ignore the naysayers and pursue your dreams. One day, the naysayers will be kissing your ring finger, wanting your favor!

Day 269

"The only person you need to try to be better than is the person you were yesterday!"

—Anonymous

Do not compare yourself to anyone else! You are one of a kind—fearfully and wonderfully created. The only person you can compare yourself to is you. Are you growing, becoming better, learning, and improving . . . each day? *That* is your only goal and only concern!

    If you compare yourself to someone else, who has a different call in their life and a different dream, you will get derailed and forget who you are. Stay focused on who you are and what your goal is in life! Ford couldn't compare himself to Edison; they were in two different fields with different goals. They had to work in different areas and ideas. Staying focused on who they were, they achieved greatness in their own areas!

    You must be like them. Stay focused on who *you* are and what *your* call in life is!

Part III: Days 201–300

Day 270

"Be fearless in the pursuit of what sets your soul on fire."

—Unknown

Ah yes, the sign of a true dreamer! Pursue your dream with fearless and reckless abandon. Pursue it like you would pursue the love of your life, knowing that without capturing it, you will never be fulfilled.

The reason so many people never reach their potential and never accomplish their dream is that they are afraid! They might start out pursuing their dream, but the trials of life soon wear them down and create fears in them. Like, fears they can't support their family, or that they might lose their job, or they might fail, or one of any number of untold fears that we feel. They let those fears tug at their confidence until they weaken and lose hope, and they then quit pursuing their dream and pursue security instead.

I can't fault anyone for that. It is a hard thing to risk what you love to pursue what sometimes only you can see. But in your later years, you sit in the chair staring blankly at the TV and thinking about what might have been. "IF!"

For those few who ran wildly and recklessly and fearlessly toward their dreams, life is an amazing adventure, and for some, it is a journey into history!

Day 271

"The impossible we do right away. Miracles just take a little longer."

—Sign in my base camp in Vietnam

We were a group of bold and optimistic young men, fighting in a faraway country. I won't say everyone had the same outlook, but by and large, we were not the downtrodden, war-weary victims that the newspapers back home tried to make us out to be. We had a sense of urgency, duty, and honor about what we were doing in Vietnam, and we worked together. We had a sense of humor, too. And we believed we could do anything. Even in the grimmest times, when death took away our comrades, we kept our spirits up by talking about how good they'd been and how we would miss them.

That sign made us feel a little invincible, and it kept us positive. I still keep that comment in my mind today, and I still try to live up to it in my daily life. I think it's a good idea!

Do the impossible every day and miracles when you can!

Day 272

"Say it: 'I believe in myself!' Say it again: 'I believe in myself!' Say it every day and believe it! What you say to yourself matters more than what anyone else says about you."

—John H. Perry

Self-talk is an important part of my daily regimen. I believe what I say to myself is *very* important and can affect me, good or bad. In the past, I caught myself muttering things like, "I'm so stupid" or "I can't get anything right." And I realized that I was subconsciously listening to myself. Now, I try to avoid those comments and make positive and reinforcing comments to myself instead.

If I mess up, I might say something like, "I messed that up, but next time, I will get it right!" Or when I am about to do something, I might say something like, "Okay, you got this; you have done it before!" I might just tell myself how great I am or how smart I am, or something like that. I do believe in being truthful. But I make it a point to have positive self-talk as often as possible because my subconscious listens to what *I* say more than what anyone else says!

Day 273

"Victory is always possible for the person who refuses to stop fighting!"

—Napoleon Hill

As a retired combat soldier (US Army Infantry, airborne, and Special Forces) and a Vietnam combat veteran, I have a strong respect for people—and especially soldiers—with the will to fight. I have a long list of people I admire. Some I have known personally, but most I have read about and studied.

At the top of my list of people I admire is a man who personifies the will to live and the will to fight to his last breath—or should I say his last spit! Master Sergeant Raul "Roy" Benavidez was a US Army Special Forces (Green Beret) soldier in Vietnam. You need to look him up and read the story of his career, especially his Medal of Honor exploits.

The key point is that, despite wounds that would have taken out most men, Benavidez fought to rescue other men until he finally collapsed and was presumed dead. Later, as the doctors were zipping him into a body bag, he summoned the strength to spit on them to let them know he was still alive. He survived thirty-seven wounds from shrapnel, knives, and bullets in a six-hour battle. He later retired from the Army and lived many years afterward, speaking to groups and encouraging people with his exploits.

Benavidez refused to quit. *You* must refuse to quit!

Part III: Days 201–300

Day 274

"The two most important days in your life are the day you are born and the day you discover why!"

—Mark Twain

You can't control the day on which you are born, but you can control what happens when you discover the reason why you were born! That day will be the day you realize your goal, your dream, and the purpose you have in life. Be it a profession, a calling, or a dream to create something, it is why you exist!

You then must decide whether you are going to follow that purpose or instead lead an average life. Far too many people find reasons why they can't achieve their purpose, and they drift into average, losing the opportunity to the status quo instead of reaching for the stars and going for the dream!

I know the list of why you can't. But the list of why you *should* is more compelling:

1. The road less traveled is far less crowded.
2. The road less traveled has the fewest competitions.
3. The road less traveled has greater rewards.
4. The road less traveled is far more exciting.
5. The other road is always accessible, so you aren't missing anything if you try the road less traveled.
6. And the best is that . . . you might succeed!

Try the road less traveled for a while. You might find you like it. After all, it's why you were born!

Day 275

"Once you learn to quit, it becomes a habit!"

—Vince Lombardi

It's easier to learn a bad habit than a good habit. And quitting is definitely a *bad* habit!

The difference between those who become champions and those who don't is the habit of quitting. People like Michael Jordan never quit. They kept trying and practicing until the difficult was routine.

I once read about a man who went to a driving range before playing golf, and there were two pro golfers practicing their pitching wedge shots while he was warming up. He said he went out and played eighteen holes, and afterward, he went back to the range to work on his driver. The two pros were still there and still working on their wedge shots. He said that is when he realized the real difference between the average golfer and a pro: pros don't quit!

Day 276

"Focus on your progress, not on what is not working!"

—Unknown

Sometimes, we get obsessed with what's not working and lose sight of what is. When we are pursuing a goal, we have to stay focused on the goal and what we are really pursuing!

In all of Edison's experiments to find the best filament for the light bulb, his team didn't try to improve the filaments that didn't work. Instead, they went for new ideas that would work. If they had fixated on trying to improve the materials that weren't working instead of finding ones that would, they might have spent years longer finding the right solution or . . . missed it outright.

Stay focused on your actual goal and follow the plan!

Day 277

"The negative mind finds fault in everything, while a positive mind sees opportunity in everything."

—Unknown

So true! A negative person will always see the dark cloud in any situation, while a positive person will see the silver lining in every situation.

When I am in a situation where I have a group helping me, I usually like to have a slightly negative type in the group. Why? I know that there will be problems, and too often, all positive minds will overlook things that end up sidelining progress. So, I like having that one negative person who will point out the potential problems early on so that we can plan for them in advance.

Still, I want mostly positive types who see solutions over problems. It is true that even positive people will often see the problems. But they see them as obstacles to be overcome rather than barriers to progress. And remember that sometimes, the obstacle can be a positive and might be a step up rather than a step back!

Part III: Days 201–300

Day 278

"You might feel down because you are in a valley, but remember that to get to the next peak, you have to cross through the valleys!"

—John H. Perry

Watch the waves at the beach. They come in crests and troughs, not in one continuous crest. And the stock market climbs in peaks and valleys. The progress is tracked by the midline progress, not any single valley or peak. And when you travel from mountain top to mountain top, you have to descend into the valleys in between to climb to the next peak.

So, don't despair when you are in a valley. It only means you are ready to climb the next peak—it is the next opportunity to rise higher! Once you have reached one peak, you cannot go higher without going to another mountain. So, rejoice when you cross the valleys because new opportunities await!

Day 279

"The measure of intelligence is the ability to change."

—Albert Einstein

I know numerous people with bachelor's degrees. I know multiple people with master's degrees. I know a lot of people with PhDs and those who are for real doctors and lawyers. All of them are well-educated and highly educated. BUT not all of them are intelligent! Argue if you will but educated does not mean intelligent. Some of the highest-educated (PhDs, etc.) and those with master's degrees and bachelor's degrees are just educated idiots. All they can do is regurgitate what their professors fed them. They are close-minded and will not think for themselves. Any new ideas or discussions beyond what they learned in school, and they are unable to function!

Without the ability to take what you learn and apply it to reality, accept the facts that change, and realize that all you learned is not locked in concrete, you are doomed to fail in life. You are also not truly intelligent! None of our greatest inventions came about with conventional wisdom.

Day 280

"The risk you're afraid to take could be the one that changes your entire life!"

—Kylie Francis

Sometimes, we balk at taking a risk not because we are afraid of failing but because we are afraid of succeeding. Success will change your life! You can't go back when you succeed; you must remain committed to going forward.

Regardless of the why, the risk you avoid might be the one that radically changes your life forever. When you face a new challenge and find yourself balking at the venture, ask yourself what about it is causing you to hesitate. Is it too dangerous physically, or emotionally, or financially? Or does it hold the possibility of changing the course of your life for the better? When you realize what it is about the challenge that creates hesitation in you, then you can better judge how to approach the challenge.

Never be afraid to let something change your life, especially if it is obviously for the better!

Day 281

"If you are tired of starting over, stop giving up!"
—Unknown

Whoa, does this hit home! It hit me right between the eyes. How many times had I quit and then started over? Too often, we do it and don't even realize what we are doing. We make plans and let other things deter us from following up, and then we start over again.

Even if you have to manage multiple irons in the fire, don't repeatedly quit and start over! Keep at the tasks you feel are important and follow through on them. Make time for them. If you can make time to watch a football game or a movie, then make time for the items that matter to your life and see that they are finished.

There are somethings that don't have to take your whole attention. You can give them a portion of your time, and they will grow, like a flower. You plant a flower and water it, spend a few minutes a day taking care of it, and it flourishes over time. Some ideas or businesses are like that; they only require a small amount of your time to grow.

If you ignore the flower altogether, it dies, and you have to start over. So, don't ignore it. Instead, give it the few minutes a day it warrants and enjoy its growth!

Day 282

"Great works are performed not by strength but by perseverance!"

—Samuel Johnson

Ever watch ants build their mounds? They don't accomplish it with great moments of effort but by slow, persistent effort. Each worker brings forth a grain at a time and stacks it slowly until the ants have completed their mound.

That's how great works are accomplished—by perseverance! It's not a dash but rather a marathon. Some works are completed faster than others. But in their own ways, each takes time. Like great relationships, they are built step by step, day by day, incident by incident and cemented with experience and interaction.

Don't rush into your purpose expecting to see it unfold overnight. It will take time, it will take nurturing, and it will need patience. Anything of quality does.

Day 283

"No person can climb beyond the limitations of their own belief!"

—Myles Munroe

I mentioned Roger Bannister and the four-minute mile earlier in this book. The time restraint was a good example of a self-imposed restraint—one put on runners by the limit of their own beliefs. The runners could come within seconds of breaking the four-minute mile but never broke it until Bannister did. And within the few weeks thereafter, numerous other runners passed the mark as well because the "belief barrier" was broken!

We can unnecessarily limit ourselves so easily. Just thinking we can't is enough to guarantee we won't! Why? Because when we get close to achieving something, our subconscious will take over and stop us from going any further.

In the movie *Facing the Giants*, there is a scene where a coach blindfolds a player and has him do a death crawl without knowing how far he is actually going. The player goes twice as far as he thinks he is capable of. Granted, it is a movie, but it is a great example of what we are talking about today. If our belief system is blocked out of the picture, we can achieve much more than we realize!

Stop setting your limits before you start, and instead, just see how far you can actually go. You will amaze yourself!

Day 284

"Success isn't always about greatness. It's about consistency. Consistent hard work gains success, and greatness will follow!"

—Dwayne Johnson

People want to think success always denotes greatness, but that's not so. Greatness is measured by people's attitudes or societies' rankings, but success is defined by the achievement of a goal. You can be successful by being the best garbage man but not considered great by societal norms (whether rightly or wrongly).

If you set out to achieve a goal—a dream—and you achieve that goal, then you have achieved success. You might not be deemed "great," but you are still a success! People usually don't like this idea because recognition as great satisfies the ego, and that is what most people really seek. But the ones who are willing to work hard usually aren't concerned with ego; they want to achieve a goal!

Day 285

"Don't give up when you can't see results right away. Some things take time. Just be patient with yourself!"

—Unknown

Many great breakthroughs have come after the person thought they had failed. Medical tests have been tried and thought unsuccessful, but when done another day, they showed to be real successes. For example, Penicillin was discovered after what appeared to be a failure.

Sometimes, we rush things, not knowing how long a reaction is going to take. When you apply for a loan, the process may take longer than you hoped because it has to go through higher levels in the financial organization. But don't give up until you get a no. And if you get a no, don't even give up then! Instead, ask why, and then re-apply there or somewhere else.

Everyone won't see the outcome you see or the real-world effects of your dream, so be patient about their comprehension of what your plan entails. You might have to locate the right backers or the right supporters to get it rolling!

Part III: Days 201–300

Day 286

> "A wise man makes his own decisions; an ignorant man follows public opinion."
>
> —Chinese Proverb

Wow! This one flies in the eyes of popular modern opinion. Most people today seem to think you should comply with the status quo. But if you are going to make a breakthrough or create a new thing, you might have to buck the system!

Sometimes, you will have to be a rebel in society's eyes. If you take a step back and look at who the leading person in industry or technology is today, you will be looking at the rebels of thirty or forty years ago! Bezos, Jobs, and Gates were all "rebels" in their start-up days. Few people took them seriously. When Frederick W. Smith started FedEx, people laughed at him. Not now, though! None of them listened to public opinion; they all made their own decisions.

I would advise making your own decisions on your dreams like the people mentioned today did!

Day 287

"When life gets hard, don't wish it to be easier, decide to be stronger."

—Unknown

It's when life is easy that we get weak. And that is the real issue with society today! Many of today's youth have life relatively too easy. They can't face reality, and they demand "safe places" when faced with the truth. Instead of seeing history as a lesson to learn from, they run from it and want to tear it down and destroy it because it scares them. What *should* scare today's youth is that history is repeating itself, and they don't recognize it because they are running around hiding in their safe places.

You must face hard truths, experience hard times, and get your hands dirty to get tougher. Get tough, people—play in the dirt!

Part III: Days 201–300

Day 288

"Great things never came from comfort zones!"
—Unknown

Well said! Too many people won't get one inch outside of their comfort zone.
    I don't like that color. I don't like that neighborhood. I don't like that texture. I don't like . . . Well, *have you even tried any of it*?
    People who think like that remind me of little children saying, "I don't like spinach." Have you ever eaten Spinach? "No, I don't like it!" Just try one mouthful, and if you don't like it, I will never ask you to try it again. And it's amazing how many actually *like* spinach!
    I can attest to that. I didn't like asparagus for thirty years until my wife had me actually eat it. And now it's one of my favorites!
    Get out of your comfort zone. It's fun out here! It's exciting, and you will discover new things and new ways. You might even . . . like spinach!

Day 289

"Mindset is everything!"

—Unknown

How you see your world is all about your mindset! No lie. The reason you and I see things differently is because we have different mindsets. It's not that I am right and you are wrong (even if you are), but we have a different mindset and therefore perceive things in a different light. It might be a very subtle or extreme difference in mindset, but there is a difference.

Say we are watching television and a commercial comes on, and there is a scene promoting a shampoo, and there are two people of the same sex as the parents washing a child's hair with the shampoo. If I am unbiased to the LGBT movement, then I am more focused on the shampoo's qualities. But if you are anti-LGBT, then you are focusing on the LGBT side of the commercial and are biased against the shampoo because of that. It is a silly reaction, but it is a function of mindset, and it might lose the shampoo company a customer.

Mindset influences how you see your world. What is *your* mindset?

Day 290

"If you are not willing to learn, no one can help you! If you are determined to learn, no one can stop you!"

—Zig Ziglar

This is a statement that I would have expected from someone like Socrates or Aristotle, but instead, it comes from the great Zig Ziglar! Once a person has determined they know something, they are no longer willing to learn the truth. Too often, that is the seat of the problem in society, especially in select groups or segments of society. People get information from sources they believe and then refuse to accept contrary information, and their learning is blocked.

For example, a group puts out information about a historical figure that creates a negative image, and people begin pushing for that person to be banned from the education system because of that information. However, true historians bring up facts that show that information to be incorrect, and they promote the truth, but the segment pushing for banishment refuses to listen, and the education system goes along with the misinformed. That is going on today, at the time of this writing. There are people unwilling to learn and unwilling to teach truth.

If someone is willing to learn, they will seek any and all sources for truth and information, they will disregard lies and rumors, and they will look at all facets of the story!

Day 291

"'Someday' is a disease that will take your dreams to the grave with you!"

—Unknown

"Someday, I will pursue my dream." That is a fitting epitaph for many a headstone! Far too many great works or ideas have gone to the grave unfollowed, unpursued, and unfulfilled. Dead people accomplish nothing. And dead goals also accomplish nothing.

If 10 percent of people with dreams would just rise up and pursue their dreams, our world would be an astonishing place! Even if you start it as a part-time venture, get off your couch and start exploring the call you have for your life. What is it that flicks your Bic? What is it that you used to dream of and now wish you had gone for? It's not too late; give it a shot!

Day 292

"Winning has a price. Leadership has a price. I pushed people when they didn't want to be pushed. I challenged people when they didn't want to be challenged. But I never asked them to do something I wasn't willing to do myself."

—Michael Jordan

The real challenge is leading *yourself*, pushing *yourself*, challenging *yourself*, and asking *yourself* to do the hard things! Michael Jordan didn't get where he was by being average. Instead, he was already a champion in his own right, and when he started leading, he had already set the bar high. Will you challenge yourself? Will you be your own leader and motivate yourself? No one can do it for you because if they do, then you are a follower, not a leader!

It takes being a leader to chase your dream. Lead yourself to greatness—motivate yourself! Earlier in this book, I presented the idea of self-talk. Give yourself pep talks. Tell yourself how great you are and how great you are going to be. Push yourself to keep going. Congratulate yourself and set new goals when you achieve your old ones. *You* are your biggest fan!

Day 293

"Don't limit your challenges, challenge your limits."

—Unknown

Do you know how you reach new limits? By pushing past the ones you reach! Sounds too simple to be true, but that's all there is to it!
When I was young, I used to work out with weights a lot. I set goals for the weight I wanted to reach when doing each exercise, like curls, presses, and bench presses. When I got to those goals, I was happy for a while. But soon, I felt like I needed to move on. I realized that all I had to do was just add a few pounds to each exercise, and when I was comfortable with it, add more . . . and so on! Pretty soon, I was amazing myself and my friends with my strength. All it took was to push past my limits a little bit at a time.

You can do that in anything you do! As I mentioned earlier in this book, we set our own limits with our beliefs. If we accept that as true, then when we reach a limit, we can change our beliefs and exceed that limit!

Try it. What's the area you feel limited in? What will it take to push past that limit? What belief will you have to change, and what action will you have to take to change that limit? *Do it!*

Day 294

"You are always one decision away from a totally different life."

—Unknown

I met my wife at an ice-skating rink. She walked in one Monday, just as we were starting a group skating lesson, and I asked the pro to give her a free lesson—one that I would pay for. He said this was going to spell trouble because I was dating other ladies from the rink at the time! But I said, "No problem. I have it all under control." Ha!

By Wednesday, I had made a fateful decision that was I was going to marry her! My only challenge was, how was I going to convince her to marry me? I wasn't sure she even liked me. I might also mention that, by this time, the other ladies were history, and my only thoughts were of my future wife. My plans when my wife came into my life were simplistic and typically chauvinistic, but by the end of the week, I had thrown them all to the wind and changed my whole future plan—all from assuming she would marry me.

That one decision—to pursue my future wife—literally altered my whole future, and I have never regretted it. As a matter of fact, it was the best decision I have ever made outside of salvation.

What decision is going to change *your* life?

Day 295

"You want to change your life? Change the way you think!"

—Unknown

The fact is, you cannot change anything about your life until you change the way you think! You can try. But like a rubber band, you will stretch until you reach your limit and then snap back to what you were before. You are what you think, and you will *react* as you think!

If you have a poverty mentality, then you can make all the money you want, but you will be poor at the core and be grasping for money, even when you have more than enough. If you are unthankful, you will not appreciate people or things and will not be likable. You have to change how you think and what you think so that you are properly oriented to life.

Think successfully if you want to be successful. And be grateful for what you have and for those in your life. Have a giving spirit and share your success with those who help you.

Day 296

"Other people may quit on you, but you have to make sure you never quit on yourself!"

—Christopher Ferry

The one true thing you can count on is that you can't always count on other people! And sadly, this might even apply to those who you most expect to be there for you. You must be prepared to have people walk out on you, stab you in the back, or quit on you. They might not even mean you harm. They might just not be able to hang in there for the long haul.

Regardless of who else or what else occurs in your life, do not quit on yourself! One reason is that *you* are the one with the dream, not them. Another reason is that some people might be looking to you and will recover and rejoin you if you keep on. No matter what, *you* are the central person in this drama, and the story only ends if you do. You can always come back for those who grew tired, but *you* have to finish!

Day 297

"Being defeated is often a temporary condition. Giving up is what makes it permanent."

—Marilyn vos Savant

This is a distinction that many people don't realize! Defeat is temporary, but accepting defeat makes it permanent. That's called giving up.

You always risk defeat when you try something, especially something new or difficult. But when you face defeat, just call it a failure, and you know from earlier in this book that you must learn from it and try again using the lesson learned. In contrast, giving up is called quitting, and quitters *never* win. So, quitting is *not* an option!

Part III: Days 201–300

Day 298

"I think anything is possible if you have the mindset, and the will, and the desire to do it, and you put the time in!"

—Roger Clemens

Roger Clemens is a world-class baseball pitcher, and like other athletes I have referenced throughout this book, he has spent his life working hard and long to perfect his skills. He knows that the same efforts he put into becoming a hall of fame pitcher can be used to become almost anything he wants to be.

You can be a great engineer, doctor, stock trader, teacher, actor, whatever, if you have the right mindset, will, and desire to do it and put in the time! Everyone needs to grasp this simple concept in life. This is how you succeed at whatever you want to do. Consistency, persistency, and dedication!

Day 299

> "Things won't always go your way. Be mature enough to accept that."
>
> —Unknown

Sometimes, people get frustrated and quit because things don't go their way. Really, people? Things not going your way is life. So, if everyone quit when things didn't go their way, the world would be a totally different and much worse place today. George Washington and the patriots would have just gone home and said to heck with it if they'd had that attitude. I know Valley Forge wasn't on their agenda!

Most ventures will face disappointment and frustration at many points along the way. There's that old saying: "The best-laid plans of mice and men . . ." Well, as already discussed many times in this book, sometimes, the fact that things don't go your way can be the best thing that happens to you!

I read that when they were shooting the movie *Jaws*, the opening scene was supposed to have the shark appear in it, but the mechanical shark broke down. So, they had to improvise by making the opening music more dramatic. And it turns out that the music made the opening scene the most traumatic and greatest of all time. I still don't like the first five minutes of the movie because of that terrifying music! The director, Steven Spielberg, could have thrown a fit and done something else, but instead, he improvised, and it worked to his benefit.

Live with it. Whatever "it" is might be the best thing that happens to you!

Part III: Days 201–300

Day 300

"Giving up something now for something better later is not a sacrifice. It is an investment."

—Unknown

Short-term sacrifice for long-term gain: the staple of life's wealth builder! Invest in your future. Time, finances, whatever it takes, invest in your future. So many people expend everything for the now and have nothing for the tomorrow!

A career is a long-term investment. You invest in a company or a profession for what it will bring to your future security. People who drift from job to job don't have long-term security. If you invest in a dream, a goal, something that holds a future, it is an investment for the long-term, not short-term!

I am always frustrated with people who begrudge a business owner for what they have built, claiming that the workers made the business. No, the business gave the workers a job, and the owner created the business, so the owner created the work for the workers; they didn't create the wealth for the owner! The owner could have hired anyone. The owner created the business, and when it became successful, the owner should reap the reward. The workers didn't risk anything to start or build the business; they were and are liabilities, not assets.

The owner invested for the future—for the long-term. And once the long-term is reached, the owner provides for the workers.

PART IV

~DAYS 301–366~

Day 301

"Learning is the only thing the mind never exhausts, never fears, and never regrets."

—Leonardo da Vinci

The mind is created to learn. From birth, we learn. Every experience is a learning experience.

What we do as we get older is controlled by our environment and how we decide to use our minds. Many people will use their minds only to survive. Some will use it to create, to explore the world, or to teach. And others will use their minds to reach beyond their own limits to search for answers to the mysteries of the universe.

Each mind is capable of great things and is limited only by the person using it! How will you use *your* mind?

Day 302

"Stop being ashamed of how many times you have fallen and start being proud of how many times you have gotten back up!"

—Unknown

This quote is a slight variation of what was said way back on Day 9 and is worth repeating. We *all* fall. What matters is how many times we get back up and what we do when we get up! If we fall ten times, then we must get back up at least ten times. And each time, we must start again, reaching for the greatness we are designed for.

Falling is just a sign that we are striving, not a sign of weakness! Falling is a lesson—we learn what not to do. And the next time we reach the obstacle that tripped us up, we avoid it. We might fall again because of a new obstacle, but we rise and learn again!

Watch a baby learning to walk. They don't fall after one attempt and never try again. They keep at it, determined to accomplish the task. And soon, they are not only walking, they are running. They still fall, but they get up faster and move quicker.

Go ahead, fall if you have to but rise and run!

Day 303

"Everything comes to you at the right time. Be patient!"

—Unknown

My sixteen-year-old comes to me and asks for the keys to the car, and I hand them over. Next, my ten-year-old comes to me and asks for the keys to the car, and I say not yet. Unfair? No. It's not the ten-year-old's time yet. In a few more years, after they pass their driving test, they will get the keys, too. But at the right time!

Everyone will get what they need at the right time for them! Patience is necessary during your pursuit of your dreams. If your dream is to be a great surgeon, and you are eleven and in the sixth grade, you will need to finish your education and the proper schooling for the degrees and training you need for that profession. You might be brilliant and accelerate through what you need. But you will still need to follow the normal progression. So, be patient!

No matter how good you think you are, it's important that you get everything you need in the order you need it. If you try to skip a step or accelerate your progress beyond your true capabilities, it might endanger others, or you, or your future career. Trust the system and pursue your dream correctly.

Day 304

"There is only one way to succeed at anything, and that is to give it everything."

—Unknown

Again, this is a critical point. If you wish to truly succeed, you must dedicate yourself to your goals. You can't haphazardly approach your dreams and expect them to come to pass. Instead, you must be willing to aggressively pursue them. I am not saying that you can't have a life outside of your dreams. But they do need to be your top priority, and the closer you get, the more you have to focus on them.

It's like target shooting. If you just want to shoot, then hitting a target is pretty easy. But when you want to be a true marksman and hit the bullseye, you have to learn to focus and learn to practice correctly and spend more time at the range. True marksmanship doesn't come from shooting twenty rounds downrange and going out to party with your pals!

I was an excellent pistol shooter at one point in my military career, spending many hours a week at the range. But I was not a high-quality competitor because I didn't spend enough time practicing. If you had seen my targets after competitions, you would have thought I was good enough. But I had seen the targets of the really good shooters, and next to them, I was pretty pathetic. They spent more time shooting in one day than I did in an entire week!

If you are serious about a dream, it takes serious dedication!

Day 305

"Stay strong, no matter how many ups and downs you go through."

—Unknown

Life is not a constant increase in success. Instead, life comes with decreases through failures, which are often not your fault or things you can anticipate.

A good example of this notion is the recurring recessions we suffer in the economy. Some are small, others large, and some almost depressions. In 2007 and 2008, a recession wiped out numerous large financial organizations and thousands of personal fortunes. People were losing their homes left and right and their businesses, too. Dreams were being crushed by debt and financial ruin, and some people never recovered.

It's easy to sit back and criticize those who never recovered from the recession. Many of them just gave up. Instead of pulling in and weathering the storm and regrouping after the recession passed, they gave up and never recovered. Their spirit was broken. Others—the strong and optimistic—regrouped, learned from what happened, and started over. Many of them are going stronger now than ever!

Be strong, and don't let the downside destroy you!

Day 306

"Don't get overwhelmed by how much time you have already wasted, and don't dwell too long on past mistakes. Just take the next step and keep the end in view."

—Francis Chan

Time that's passed can't be recouped, but past mistakes can be learned from. Now is new, and the future is not yet determined. You have a dream, a goal, and hopefully a plan. So, go for it—the time is *now*!

The first step is the next step. Even if you have tried and failed before, start again, learning from your failure. You *can* do it. The key thing is to learn from the past and adjust your plan accordingly.

Don't dwell on the past; it is gone forever. But the future is still ahead of you!

Day 307

"Some things you don't learn through advice but through adversity!"

—Unknown

The old "school of hard knocks." You often have to take a few courses and maybe even get a graduate degree at this school! Other people can tell you what they know, what they've learned, or what they've experienced. But sometimes, you have to run headfirst into the beast yourself.

 I could talk about a few things from my life that echo today's quote, but what matters is that you understand that you can't learn everything in school or from someone else's experience. You will have to go through it on your own at some point, especially if you have a unique dream you are pursuing. The Wright brothers couldn't learn some of the things they had to face because no one else had ever flown!

Day 308

"Always trust your first gut instincts. If you feel something is wrong, it usually is."

—Unknown

This is a key point and something you will need to rely on, especially in new situations and around new people. Your gut instinct is your subconscious mind telling you something. And you need to pay attention!

Sometimes, if you are working with a device, and your gut says not to do something because it's not safe, your subconscious is aware of something wrong that you consciously have overlooked. Stop, back off, and recheck everything, especially what you feel is wrong. Or, if you have a gut feeling about someone or a deal—whether good or bad—pay attention because your subconscious is aware of something you are missing. Again, step back and reevaluate what is going on.

Trust your gut instinct!

Day 309

"Never give up on a dream because of the time it will take to accomplish it. The time will pass anyway!"

—Earl Nightingale

As I previously mentioned, when I was completing my degree, I had an economics professor who was in her sixties and decided to pursue a four-year course to get her CPA. She told us that both family and friends kept telling her it was a waste of time because, by the time she completed the course, she would be almost sixty-nine. Her response when people derided her decision because she would be four years older was along these lines: "If I don't do it now, how old will I be in four years?"

No matter how long something will take, that time will still pass whether you do it or not, and if you don't do it, you will look back in regret later on. If you have a dream or desire, go for it! It's only too late if you die. I saw the economics professor some years later. By then, she was in her early seventies and had her own CPA firm and was happy as she could be.

Pursue your dreams; they are worth it at any age!

Day 310

"Progress is impossible without change, and those who cannot change their minds cannot change anything."

—Bernard Shaw

The worst obstacle to your pursuit will be . . . *you*! If you go into your venture with preconceived ideas and refuse to adapt to change, you will defeat yourself long before anything else or anyone else can.

Prejudice is often used in a race relations context, but it is applicable to anything we do. Prejudice literally means to prejudge—to form an opinion in advance. You can be prejudiced against a food, a person, a car, a school, or anything else you deal with in life. Usually, you are prejudiced by input from some other source that influences your opinions so that you do not give the object of your prejudice the option to prove itself.

Once, when my family was looking for a new car, our youngest child told us that a certain car was badly rated by a consumer magazine and that we should, therefore, not consider it. We ignored that advice and bought the car anyway, and it turned out to be one of the best cars we ever owned. Years later, she was still saying it was a badly rated car despite our experience, and she refused to own one. Her loss!

Day 311

"Straight roads do not make skillful drivers."

—Paulo Coelho

If life doesn't throw you any curves, you will never learn to handle difficulties! People whine about life's trials but fail to realize that the little things in life prepare you for the big things in life. Embrace the little trials; they are your muscle builders for the future.

Like minor diseases or germs help build a strong immune system, little trials help build a strong life-handling system. You have no idea what is coming down the road. So, take advantage of the little twists and turns to develop your driving skills now!

Day 312

"The 97 percent of people who quit are employed by the 3 percent who never gave up."

—Unknown

Yeah! And they whine because the 3 percent are making the money. They should instead be grateful that the 3 percent stayed the course; otherwise, there would be no job! Quitters are usually whiners and blame others for their problems. But if they had instead used the right attitude and stayed the course, they would be the employer instead of the employed.

Once, when I owned a small business, my workers cried about me making more than they did. I had a meeting and asked if they wanted to make an equal share. They were all in favor, so I laid out a simple proposal. I said I would split everything evenly, all they had to do was chip in and cover their share of the expenses, and I laid out what it cost to run the business. When I was through, none of them wanted in! After that, they were happy with their pay. Often, the 97 percent don't realize what the 3 percent pay out in costs!

Day 313

"If you didn't face the danger of failure today, you weren't in the game. Put yourself at risk every day."

—Unknown

You have to be in the game every day. There's no taking a break! Life is a continuous challenge. And if you are to stay a part of the challenge, you have to be at it daily.

I don't mean you have to be running the gauntlet every day. But you can't be up one day, then down the next. It's constant pursuit—the consistent effort, no matter how much—that matters. You might feel tired, but the participation will recharge you and get you going!

Day 314

> "He who knows all the answers has not been asked all the questions."
>
> —Confucius

Sometimes, the real reason someone thinks they know all the answers is just this simple; they haven't been asked all the questions! Like my grandson after graduating kindergarten ("I are graduate; I don't have to go to school anymore"), they aren't aware that there is more in life. Immaturity is usually the reason someone is so smug and so self-assured that they have all the answers. But those of us who have been around a while know there are more questions than we thought!

Day 315

"If you go out gathering honey, you can expect a few bee stings."

—Unknown

That sounds like a Middle Eastern philosophy, but actually, it is applicable to what we are talking about in this book. If you consider the honey as the resources you need or the facts you seek, you will realize that the bee stings are society's reactions to your pursuit, especially when you are not in compliance with society's idea of the norm. Think of the bee stings as the criticisms you will get for being unique or radical in your ideas. Whenever you seek something special outside of what others see as normal, they will lash out at you and your ideas. So, be prepared for their attacks!

Day 316

"It is better to be unique than to be the best. Being the best makes you number one. Being unique makes you the *only* one!"

—Unknown

And that is the pleasure of pursuing a new and special idea! Imagine being the Wright brothers, or Alexander Graham Bell, or any of the greats who came up with the first something. They are totally unique in history. It would be a great feeling. BUT it would also be frustrating because people would not see how to use your ideas.

It took some years before flight was more than a novelty in the world, and initially, aircraft were mainly war machines. And use of the telephone was highly limited at first and took years to catch on more widely. Other inventions took decades to find their niche in society.

Still, being unique is something to be desired!

Day 317

"Being alone is the secret of invention. Be alone. That is where ideas are born!"

—Nikola Tesla

This quote might not always be true, but by and large, being alone allows one to think and plan in the most peace. Tesla was so advanced that he probably couldn't do much with others around because they would question everything he did. Like Tesla, you will find yourself seeking privacy to work on your ideas and dreams because other people will question you and will want to interject their ideas—sometimes, negative ideas. Being alone lets you think clearly. Though later on, you might seek others' input, the initial planning and creation will be done alone!

Day 318

"Everyone thinks about changing the world, but no one thinks about changing himself."

—Leo Tolstoy

Sometimes, we come up with great ideas to change the world, to change society, or to change how things are done when what we really need to do is look at changing ourselves. Frequently, the system isn't broken; we are. Or our *approach* to the system is wrong.

Rather than trying to change the world, if we change how we see the world and how we interact with the world, life will improve for us and for those around us. Look inward first, and if *you* are what's wrong, then fix yourself first!

Day 319

"Education is the key to unlock the golden door of freedom."

—George Washington Carver

A very interesting man, educator, and scientist, George Washington Carver did much to further both agricultural science and black Americans' education during the early twentieth century in America. There is some folklore surrounding his life and some great scientific work he isn't widely known for. He promoted rotating crops and planting more than cotton to rebuild fields on southern farms, he took to the road to educate farmers (especially poor black farmers), and he developed numerous alternative uses for peanut products.

Even though Carver was initially denied access to white universities, he persisted and gained entrance to one and was recognized for his skills and intelligence. Later, he was appointed to Tuskegee University, where he promoted education in black communities. His impact on both black and white America in the early twentieth century was immeasurable. He truly showed that education was a key to freeing people from poverty!

Day 320

"A tiny change today brings a dramatically different tomorrow."

—Richard Bach

If you have been plugging away day after day and nothing is changing, maybe you need to make a little change in your approach! Sometimes, we get fixated with our approach and don't realize that we are doing the same thing and expecting different results. If that is the case, step back, reevaluate your process, make a little adjustment, and see what happens. Small changes now can make big changes in future results!

Day 321

"We cannot do everything at once, but we can do something at once."

—Calvin Coolidge

Sometimes, we get paralyzed because we feel we have to do it all at once. The fact is, we don't. We just have to do something—*anything*—to get the process moving!

Rather than trying to take care of the whole situation, take care of what you can. It is better to address a small portion of a project at a time anyway, allowing the project to flow gradually so that the process is controllable. Relax, take it one step at a time, and enjoy the journey!

Day 322

"When you're ready, nothing can stop you. If something's stopping you, you're not ready."

—Drew Gerald

You have to be ready to pursue your dream and ready to face the challenges associated with that pursuit. If you are not ready, you are setting yourself up for failure before you even start!

The main things that can stop you are doubt, lack of planning, and fear. While doubt and fear are intricately related, they are also separate. You can doubt your ability, or you can doubt your dream itself. You can fear failure, or you can fear success. And you can lack proper planning to begin the venture.

To be ready to pursue your dream, you must not doubt, you must not fear, and you must have some type of plan. Then, you can begin with confidence! Plans might change, but at least you have a starting point.

Day 323

"If you have haters, the solution is simple: ignore them and keep doing what you do."

—Oscar Auliq-Ice

Actually, having haters can be a *good* thing! It means what you are doing is important enough to attract someone's attention. And having haters can even motivate you.

If you let haters affect your pursuit, then it means you value other people's opinions more than your dreams, and that is not good! It's nice when people support you, but it's not essential. Not many people supported Columbus when he left for the new world, but that didn't affect his discovery at all.

Day 324

"Our dreams require us to betray who we 'should' be for who we are to become."

—Drew Gerald

This one might sound a little contradictory but think about it. We should not be what society or family think we should be. Instead, dreams dictate that we be something different than what *they* imagined!

My family believed I should be an electrician, working locally and living near them all my life. But my dreams dictated that I become a soldier, traveling the world and going to war and doing things they never imagined. My dreams made me become something I never "should" have been, according to family and friends. But it was what *I* wanted to be!

What do *you* want to be? Do you want to be the boring, cookie-cutter person that society and family see you becoming? Or would you rather be the daring, flamboyant person your dreams will make you?

Day 325

"In life, if you ever wish to see obstacles, just take your eyes off the goal."

—Previledge Tafadzwa Makaza

There's a story in the Bible in which Jesus approaches disciples in a storm by walking on water. Peter says to Jesus something like, "Lord, if you ask me, I will walk on the water too." Jesus calls him to come out of his boat, and Peter steps out and walks toward Jesus! But halfway to Jesus, Peter looks at the waves crashing around him, panics, and starts sinking in the water. He cries for Jesus to save him, and Jesus does, admonishing him not to take his eyes off Jesus.

That's exactly what today's quote is talking about. When we take our eyes off the goals of our pursuit, that's when we start seeing obstacles and problems that then start *causing* us problems. So, instead, stay focused like a *laser* on your dream, and obstacles will be few!

Day 326

"Fear will keep you grounded in the wrong way; take the leap and soar."

—Martika Shanel

Fear is like a lead weight on your feet, keeping you unable to leap in pursuit. You must shed the fear, put on wings of confidence, leap away, and soar to new heights!

You have the dream, and you've created the plan; now, start the pursuit! In due time, if you keep the faith, you will achieve your goal. Persistent effort is what you need—focused, persistent effort. Fear is doubt. Stop doubting; you *can* do it!

Day 327

"Only those who confront unusual challenges can flaunt unusual success."

—Vincent Okay Nwachukwu

To create special dreams, you have to challenge special challenges! Routine things are not going to produce special results. Not everyone will produce unique and special results. And if that realization is the challenge you face, then don't back down because it will be your chance to create special and unique results.

Only people who are thought capable of handling a challenge will be given the opportunity to do so. So, don't feel you are being taken advantage of if someone challenges you. Instead, feel blessed that you have been chosen and accept the challenge!

Day 328

"Hard work never cheats; it leads to success."

—Md Parvej Ansari

Hard work doesn't cut corners or cheat the system; it goes the full mile to achieve honest results! In order to produce the best results, a hard worker will take every step and do everything necessary to ensure total completion of a project is achieved. The final product will be of the utmost quality, ready to stand the toughest test and closest scrutiny. Once you get there, you will be able to stand proud of your work!

Day 329

"The doors of success never open to the mind shut so defiantly toward a new approach that it stops seeing or believing in the door's existence."

—Shahenshah Hafeez Khan

You have to believe in the possibilities. There are always new ways, new alternatives, and new approaches! If you close your mind to the possibilities, then you will not see the doors that are there. You will ignore the very solution or opportunity that will resolve your problem. It's a self-defeating attitude that so many create in their own mind, becoming defiantly assured that they have tried every possible solution and hardening their minds to alternatives that don't fit preconceived ideas.

Sometimes, we have to step back and clear our minds of our own ideas and let our subconscious juggle new ideas. Sometimes, we have to let our dreams show us the way because our waking mind is rebelling against a problem's solution. Don't get so fixed on the idea of what won't work that you miss seeing the solution when it is right in front of your eyes!

Day 330

"Make it happen, or it won't."

—Ronnie House Jr.

You have the dream. *You* are the one who sees it, no one else. *You* are the one called to do it. *You* are the only one who can make it a reality!

You have to make it happen, or it won't happen! Sure, someone else might come up with a similar idea, but no one will have the exact same idea you do. So, you have to make your dream a reality. If *you* don't make it happen, it will never exist!

Day 331

"Nothing worthwhile in life is gained by avoiding what is uncomfortable initially."

—Steve Lentini

In some fashion, everything starts out uncomfortable. The first day at the gym is uncomfortable. You feel out of place, awkward, and unsure of yourself. The exercises are straining and tiring, and you feel weak compared to those around you.

The first day at a new job, you are disoriented, unsure, and don't know if it will work out. You wonder if you will get the hang of all they want you to do.

On a first date, you don't know what the other person likes, how they are going to react, and whether you are acting right. Will they want to go out again? So many unknowns!

Everything is uncomfortable initially. But if it is worthwhile, you hang in there. And soon, you are comfortable, things work out, and you are good to go. Hang in there; it's going to be alright!

Day 332

"Reading refreshes as well as renews the mind."

—Lailah Gifty Akita

Sometimes, you need to stop and relax your mind. Just sit back and refresh and renew your mind. And there's nothing better than a good book for that! It can be a fiction book, nonfiction book, or even a technical book. It just needs to be something different than the subject of your pursuit in order to relax and renew your mind.

While you are reading, your mind will have time to reboot (so to speak) and "defrag" all the data you have been using the past few weeks. You will find that right in the middle of the book, you will start getting new ideas about your dream and new approaches for your pursuit. Make notes, keep reading, and let the mind go off on its own for a while longer. You'll feel so much better when you stop reading and go back to work. And you can pick up the book and read some more later on!

Day 333

"The true secret to success lies in believing in it."

—Mango Wodzak

Here is that little fact again. *Believe* in yourself, *believe* in your dream, and *believe* in your success! You have to believe in something long before you actually see it manifest. It's real; it's just not there yet!

It's like when you get in your car to drive to a faraway destination. The destination is real, and it is there. You aren't there yet, but it is real. You'll be there in time, but it is still a real place even while you are traveling to it.

Your dream is real, even while you are working to achieve it! You just aren't there . . . *yet*.

Day 334

"Don't let your fear of success keep you from it."

—Bobby Darnell

We need to keep this in mind! You have already read it in this book, but everyone tends to forget that one of the biggest fears that hinders success is the fear of success. Knowing that when you achieve success there will be responsibilities and demands places pressure on people. We wonder if we will be able to handle it or if we want to handle it. Do we want to change like these responsibilities will require us to change?

Anticipating—and sometimes, dreading—these unknowns will cause us to fail deliberately! Before we embark on the journey, we have to address this issue and make a decision. Don't get halfway and panic!

Part IV: Days 301–366

Day 335

"Success is not the key to happiness. Happiness is the key to success."

—Albert Schweitzer

Too many people equate success with happiness, and when they get there, they are disappointed because they realize they aren't happy! If you are chasing success to be happy, then you need to stop because you will end up disappointed and even more miserable if you succeed. Happy people succeed more often because they enjoy what they are doing and find pleasure in what they are achieving. When they are happy in the pursuit, they tend to be able to accept the success and the changes and grow with their success without losing themselves in the changes.

Day 336

"Today's inaction is tomorrow's reality."

—Noel Jhinku

Seem contradictory to what we are promoting? Well, let's think about it. Today's quote can be said another way: "Today's *action* is tomorrow's reality!" But inaction also becomes a reality.

If you do nothing, you achieve nothing, and you have nothing! In other words, don't just sit around doing nothing. Instead, take *action* every day. Pursue your dream, think positive, take positive action, and create a positive future. If you don't, you will create a negative, empty future!

Day 337

"To be a versatile, enterprising, successful person, one must be willing to have extreme focus and take risks when others won't."

—Germany Kent

We've said it before: focus on your goals! Like a laser sight, focus on your goals and *stay* focused. And be willing to take risks—though they should be calculated risks, for certain. Most people are too conservative in life and withhold from risk, leading sedentary lives that show little or no return. You need to get out of your comfort zone and take risks, grow beyond your limits, and expand your territory. It will pay great long-term dividends.

Day 338

"You've got to do the work no one else is willing to do in order to get the kind of success most people only dream about having."

—Jeanette Coron

The true achiever will do whatever it takes, go the extra mile, and work the longest hours to achieve success. They will do what others don't even imagine doing in order to achieve their goal. When the rest have stopped in exhaustion, collapsing on their beds for the day, the true achiever is still at work, seeking their goal with a fiery passion. And even when they stop, their minds keep at it, dreaming of the next day's process and how to do it even better. It's not a job to them; it's a passion, a love, and a way of life!

Part IV: Days 301–366

Day 339

"The very act of seeking sets things in motion."

—Laurie Buchanan

The act of stepping out of your comfort zone will set the world in motion to bring you rewards others won't get. While others are lurking in their homes and hiding in their complacency, you will be outside seeking something—anything—different and new. The very act of seeking will open new doors and attract new opportunities.

People with something to give will see you looking at new things and offer you opportunities. You will see things happening that others will miss. I can't specify exactly what to expect, but I can tell you that you will begin seeing things occur that other people will miss. People recognize special uniqueness when they see it, and when you possess it, they reach out to you!

Day 340

"If a door closes on you, and you cannot find another to open, carve out your own."

—Joy Madden

Sometimes, when someone is testing you, they will shut a door to see what you will do. If you just give up and walk away, they won't chase you. But if you kick the door in, they might have something special for you!

Maybe the first door wasn't meant for you, but there is another one or another area you fit better. Make yourself known and shove yourself in if necessary. The worst that can happen is someone tosses you out. And if that happens, then you simply go looking for something else!

Day 341

"No stress. Just keep sticking it to failure until you give birth to success."

—Curtis Tyrone Jones

When I first read this, I missed the word "it" in the phrase and almost passed it up. Then I reread it and realized what it said. Yes! Just keep sticking *it* to failure!

Every time old failure tries to trip you up, just say no. Then, come back and do it again even better. Eventually, you will get it all right, and success will be your reward!

Day 342

"Your destiny is in your hands. If you don't do anything for it, you will never be anything."

—Deb Chakraborty

The key here is that it's in *your* hands, no one else's! *You* are the master of your destiny. And *you* have to take charge.

No one is going to magically come along and say, "Here's your destiny, enjoy it!" If you let your destiny pass without doing something—without pursuing it—then it will die on the vine. You will be just another drone in the hive, serving the queen in anonymity.

Strike out and be unique. Set yourself apart and go for it!

Day 343

"Difficulties come not to obstruct but to instruct."

—Brian Tracy

Here it is again: problems are lessons, not failures and not defeats! It's important that you get this ingrained in your head from the start because no matter when or where you face difficulties, they are for your benefit, not your defeat.

It is appropriate that when you have a test in school, the questions are called "problems." They are there as teaching points. Similarly, life is a series of lessons, building you up for what you are going to face down the road. Life lessons give you what you need to overcome the next obstacles.

Take advantage of every teaching point you get!

Day 344

"Success is like an iceberg: nobody sees the work that comprises it."

—Jeffrey Fry

Boy, is this true! So many successful people do not get credit for all the work and time that went into their success. People like Michael Jordan spent decades practicing long hours alone, even after dark, on just one aspect of their game. And when they finally make it in the sport, people say things like, "They are a natural!"

A natural my butt! Jordan spent more hours practicing than you can imagine so that he could make those moves, those shots. He *isn't* a natural. He worked his rear off to be great. Or someone like Tom Hanks makes a movie, and the audience says, "He's a natural-born actor!" No, he's not. He works hard to portray those characters. He put in years to hone his craft.

Most people won't see the 90 percent of beneath-the-surface work and preparation you will put in to achieve your dream. They will only see the 10 percent that represents the final success. But to achieve that success, you must do the beneath-the-surface work and preparation!

Day 345

"Personal development is the vehicle through which success and economic growth travel."

—Nicky Verd

Though most people won't see the work and preparation you go through to achieve your success, the funny thing is that, for the most part, you will not see the personal growth and development that you will go through in the same process! You will not emerge on the other end the same person you went in as.

If you don't change and grow, you can't succeed. So, you will of natural need metamorphose into someone who is capable of handling the success you achieve. Your friends and family might realize the changes more than you, and the changes might cost you some friendships. But if you have good character, the changes will be a good thing!

Day 346

"Care the most, succeed the most."

—Maxime Lagacé

You will have to be of good character to succeed. You will have to care not only about your dream but also about other people and how your dream will affect them. As you change and as you learn to care more, you will succeed more.

Success is more than just creating something or making money. Success is also about becoming a better person. You will like who you become if you allow yourself to care!

Day 347

"The less you care about suffering and pain, the higher your chances of success and gain."

—Maxime Lagacé

It might sound scary, but suffering and pain are relative to success! A parent, especially a mother, knows much about suffering and pain. She will put up with whatever it takes to see her children prosper. Childbearing and childbirth are often about suffering and pain. It's a good thing that women are the mothers as men would not well-tolerate what mothers do!

In a sense, motherhood is a good example of pursuing a dream because you have to bear the dream inside you, nurture it, and give birth to it! Then, you have to raise it and protect it.

Can *you* be a mother?

Day 348

"Decide to believe in yourself. Be patient and strong because there is no doubt you possess the ability to overcome obstacles throughout your life."

—Aurora Berill

We never realize how many obstacles we have faced and overcome until we stop and look back at our lives. We take things for granted, especially the day-to-day obstacles. But each of us has faced many obstacles, even if we don't realize it! Some obstacles we took in stride because they were a part of something we wanted or liked, but they were still obstacles.

How we face an obstacle is more about attitude than about what the obstacle is. When you wanted your driver's license, you didn't mind the written test or the driver's test because it had a reward you desired. But the final exam in English class was a different story; it was a pain in the neck.

Overcoming obstacles is all about perspective and attitude!

Day 349

"Think about your future in a positive way, and you will move toward your goals."

—Aurora Berill

This is key to life! Despite what we think, too often, we move forward in life with a sense of dread rather than positive excitement. It's because we are uncertain what the future holds and are afraid of failure that we have this lingering dread. No one can know what the future holds, but we *can* have a more positive outlook if we have positive goals and plans!

I think too many young people are moving forward on plans made by their family rather than by them. And when that is the case, I can understand dreading a future you don't want. You must take control of your life and plan what *you* want, even if you have to go out on your own!

Day 350

"Achieving success is difficult, but each time you focus on your goal, you get closer. Believe it; you shall achieve your destiny."

—Dele Andersen

Like I said on an earlier day, you have to be reaching for the life and goal that *you* want, not what someone else has planned for you. It is fine to want to follow in your family business or a family career, but if you do so, ensure it is *your* choice. Don't get pushed into it just because! There is nothing worse than having the dream of being a sailor and being pushed into a life as a lawyer. You would never be happy.

Day 351

"Listen with intent to learn."

—Cindy Ann Peterson

The better part of conversation is being a good listener. When you listen, pay attention, and learn from what you hear. If you are in good company, there is usually a lot to be learned from the people you are in conversation with!

When I was a young enlisted soldier, my job was to carry the radio for my platoon leader. I listened to his radio conversations—to the operations orders—and when we attended meetings, to the conversations at the meetings. By the time I was promoted out of the radio job, I knew how to be a platoon leader and do operations orders because I had listened and learned. From there, being a squad leader was easy!

In social conversations, you can learn who to contact for a number of things, who is in charge, where to go for needs, etc. So, listen and learn!

Day 352

"It takes courage to be a successful entrepreneur. Thus, courage is the parent of success."

—Jawo

There is one main reason most people don't become entrepreneurs: they are afraid! Afraid of risk. Afraid of losing money. Afraid of lawsuits. Afraid of no income. Afraid of not getting work or customers. Afraid of economic downturn. And the list goes on and on!

It's easier to work for somebody else than to work for yourself. But I *like* working for myself! Typically, I can make more in an hour for myself than I can in a day for someone else. Plus, I can control my hours!

My wife says I am a bad businessman because I don't charge enough. But I tell her I can sleep at night, especially when it comes to providing for old people. If you can't be in business for yourself, that's okay. But if you can, it's fun!

Day 353

"If you see a dedicated and hardworking person, you've seen someone closer to success. Never give up."

—Dele Andersen

A good work ethic is a rare commodity. If you've got one, then welcome to the world of successful people! Today's world is full of people who want a paycheck but don't want to earn it. The sad thing is that most businesses don't reward the ones who work like they should.

In 2020, I went through a fast-food restaurant in Destin, Florida, and the line was slow. When I got to the window to pay, I discovered that the lady at the window was the *only* person working! She was taking the orders, cooking the food, and handling the window and had been doing so since opening at 6 a.m. By then, it was almost noon. I asked if she was getting paid extra, and she said no. Her boss should have been horse-whipped. She deserved a bonus! I would have hired her out from under him if I had needed a good worker.

Day 354

"Successful people are products of successful habits."

—Sesan Kareem

Habits dictate the end result of your life. On an earlier day, we had a quote from Napoleon Hill that said: "Both success and failure are largely the results of habit." This is so, so true!

If you want to be successful, you must develop successful habits. Be on time. Be persistent. Complete tasks. Have integrity. Be consistent. These and more are all good habits!

Any habit, good or bad, can be broken or developed in six weeks. Decide what you want and create a plan to develop or break the habit. Follow the plan and stick with it day after day.

Once you have established a habit, you will automatically do it every day!

Day 355

"One's success can only be achieved with abundant failures."

—Yasmina Haque

I won't say this is 100 percent fact, but if you study all the great inventors and such, you will find that they suffered numerous failures and setbacks. We don't hear a lot about the failures and setbacks because the person ultimately succeeded. But facts are facts: they overcame a lot of difficulties along the way!

It's a shame that history washes over the difficulties so often because it hides the real story. Suffice it to say, you will have a tough row to hoe, but it is well worth it, and the end is what everyone will remember! And like so many, once you succeed, you will be called "lucky," a "natural," or some other name that hides all the hard work you put in.

Day 356

"There is success, and there is failure. The land in-between is for those too weak to live."

—Sabaa Tahir

The land in-between is for those who never try. Everyone who tries will not succeed. Sorry, but that's a truth. Even the best might fail, and not because they don't try but simply because not everyone will succeed. But don't use that as a reason not to try because you don't know who will fail, and it might not be you!

It is better to have tried and failed than to have never tried at all! Failure is not total defeat. Failure just means that for your dream, it wasn't your time. There are numerous failures in the history books. The failures are just not recorded as prominently as the great successes. One thing is for sure . . .

There are no "never-trieds" in the history books!

Day 357

"More often than not, the secret of success lies in the very basic, the very small, wins. The small, consistent, and disciplined steps lead to big successes."

—Abhishek Ratna

I used to teach classes on setting goals, and the main thing I taught was setting a series of goals. Too often, a person sets a goal and just sets out. Take, for example, a goal of, "I want to get a degree in business." Depending on where you are, that can be a long and trying climb. If you don't even have a high school degree, that is a long climb.

I taught people to set the goal more achievable by breaking the long-term goal down into a series of smaller goals. For example, let's say someone's long-term goal is to get a bachelor's in engineering, which takes a total of four to six years. One short-term goal on the way would be to get a high school degree or equivalency first, which takes only six months to two years. The next short-term goal would be to get an associate degree, which takes only two to three years. By achieving those short-term goals first, you will set yourself up for achieving your long-term goal.

Celebrate and adjust as you reach each intermediate goal. You will see progress as you reach each level!

Day 358

"If you want to reach the heights of success, then step up and never look back."

—Gaurav IITM

The way to the top of the mountain is up! Sometimes, you have to go down to go up. But the purpose of the climb is always to ascend.

It will get tougher as you go, and you will get tired. But if you want to reach the peak, then you only have one choice. One choice: keep climbing! There's nothing better than reaching the peak, looking out over the horizon, and knowing you have achieved victory!

Day 359

"Celebrating the small wins is a great way to build confidence and start feeling better about yourself."

—Abhishek Ratna

Big victories are great, but they are usually few and far between. Small ones come more often and are easier to get. And . . . they add up!

Celebrate your small victories! As today's quote says, they give you confidence. And they lead to bigger and better victories. And if the small victories are related, then they add up to create a big victory. Wars are won through a *series* of battles!

Day 360

"Act and fail, but don't fail to act."

—Amit Kalantri

Self-explanatory! As we have said many times so far, the reason so many dreams are never fulfilled is that the person never pursued the dream! Whatever the reason—and we have addressed many reasons so far in this book—failure to simply act is so often the sole cause of overall failure.

I noted early on in this book that I invented a few things decades ago in my mind and on paper but never did anything with them. Then, years later, I saw essentially the same ideas for sale in magazines. The difference between my inventions and those ones was that someone took action to make them a reality!

My grandson's favorite saying used to be, "Coulda, woulda, shoulda." That says it all!

Day 361

"Don't hesitate to give up the better to gain the best."

—Amit Kalantri

One problem I see and that I admittedly have myself is that we tend to get satisfied with the better and stop working toward the best. In other words, we accept what's good enough instead of pushing for what's best!

In pioneer days, that was the experience many settlers had as they grew tired of pushing west and settled in "acceptable" lands instead of pushing on to the really good lands ahead. I suppose it's probably just as well in some cases, or there wouldn't be towns in much of the western states.

In your pursuit of a dream, don't grow weary and get satisfied with "good enough." Instead, push on and create the *best*! It only takes a little more effort.

Day 362

"Without vision, there is no victory."

—Lailah Gifty Akita

Some of the greatest battles in history have been won by unconventional thinking. In the Bible, we read about a battle where Solomon was being attacked by a superior force, but by using the terrain around him and polished shields, he blinded the attacking forces by reflecting sunlight into their eyes with the shields. This caused the attacking forces not to realize that they were headed into a chasm between them and Solomon's position. Before they realized what was happening, most of their force had perished by falling to their death!

Solomon's approach was an unconventional use of terrain and natural resources to defeat an enemy. He used his imagination (his vision) to come up with the idea. Likewise, you must use your vision to conceive the plan and the direction of your pursuits!

Day 363

"Too much thought into the process kills innovation and at times, the outcome altogether."

—Torron-Lee Dewar

Too much thinking might cause you to stifle the creative juices—the out-of-the-box ideas that you need to see the real solution. Many new ideas need to be approached with an open mind and with the understanding that it's never been done and old answers might not apply. Imagination rather than logic might be the most important viewpoint!

When Leonardo da Vinci drew the diagram of a flying machine, he wasn't using conventional thinking or scientific ideas of the time. Instead, he was using his imagination and creative thinking *outside* the scientific ideas of his time.

Too much thinking can sometimes limit your solution!

Day 366

"Living is different from just existing."
—Joshua Suya Pelicano

True living is exploring all of your options and going well beyond your comfort zone! Anyone can "just exist" in life, but only a few will really live.

It doesn't matter what your lot in life is, there are adventures waiting to stimulate your senses, challenge your imagination, and push your daring to the extreme. The adventures might be physical, or they might be mental, or maybe even emotional, but they are there, and you need to find them. Stimulate yourself at all levels and stay aware of your environment. Take advantage of the opportunities that present themselves and see where you can go in pursuit of your destiny.

LIVE life!

Conclusion

YOU'VE REACHED THE END of a full year's worth of positive and motivational sayings and discussions. Now, you can either start the book over again or find a new list of motivators. Regardless, write down quotes that most inspire you, and put them up where you will see them each day—your bathroom mirror, your refrigerator, your wallet, your desk at work, etc.

Remind yourself of your self-worth and keep up your positive self-talks! You have only just begun your journey, and you must keep at it because the world is full of negatives that are waiting to fill your mind if you let them. But *you* alone control how you see each day and each event in each day. So, think positive, take positive actions, and enjoy positive outcomes!

It never hurts to reread something and refresh your thoughts. So, I encourage you to, from time to time, reopen this book and read from a favorite section or pick a day at random. You need positive input daily, just as you need daily exercise.

I can tell you that writing this book has been a real pick-me-up for me. And I pray it has been as much so for you to read it. Once you get positive and start taking positive actions, life begins improving immediately.

Happy living!

From the Publisher

Thank You from the Publisher

Van Rye Publishing, LLC ("VRP") sincerely thanks you for your interest in and purchase of this book.

VRP hopes you will please consider taking a moment to help other readers like you by leaving a rating or review of this book at your favorite online book retailer. You can do so by visiting the book's product page and locating the button for leaving a rating or review.

Thank you!

Resources from the Publisher

Van Rye Publishing, LLC ("VRP") offers the following resources to readers and to writers.

For *readers* who enjoyed this book or found it useful, please consider receiving updates from VRP about new and discounted books like this one. You can do so by following VRP on Facebook (at www.facebook.com/vanryepub), Twitter (at www.twitter.com/vanryepub), or Instagram (at www.instagram.com/vanryepub).

For *writers* who enjoyed this book or found it useful, please consider having VRP edit, format, or fully publish your own book manuscript. You can find out more and submit your manuscript at VRP's website (at www.vanryepublishing.com).

Thank you again!

www.ingramcontent.com/pod-product-compliance
Lightning Source LLC
Chambersburg PA
CBHW072001150426
43194CB00008B/956